T0339414

DESIGNING
FOR DEPTH
IN THE
CLASSROOM

Differentiate your gifted classroom by designing experiences instead of writing lesson plans with *Designing for Depth in the Classroom: A Framework for Purposeful Differentiation.*

Addressing the specific needs of countless gifted learners doesn't have to be overwhelming and unsustainable! In her dynamic new book, Andi McNair guides readers through a fresh mindset and process for designing meaningful experiences that leave gifted learners engaged, empowered, and motivated to move from surface-level learning to deep understanding. Chapters cover topics such as project-based learning, authentic engagement, supporting and encouraging learners in the classroom and beyond, and the many ways to provide depth, with space provided at the end of each chapter for reflection questions and key takeaways.

With practical strategies, advice, and examples imparted in a refreshing conversational tone, this valuable resource is required reading for all educators interested in challenging and exciting their students in a meaningful and manageable way.

Andi McNair was a classroom teacher in public education for 16 years before pursuing her passion to change education by sharing practical ways to engage and empower today's learners as an international speaker/consultant. She is the author of *Genius Hour, Ready-to-Use Resources for Genius Hour in the Classroom*, and *A Meaningful Mess*, and is currently a Digital Innovation and Gifted/Talented Specialist at ESC Region 12 in Waco, Texas, USA.

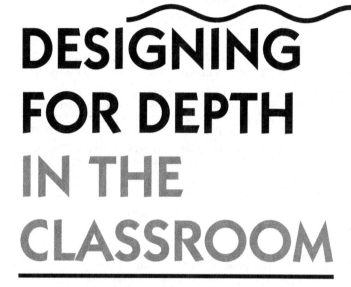

DESIGNING
FOR DEPTH
IN THE
CLASSROOM

A FRAMEWORK FOR
PURPOSEFUL DIFFERENTIATION

Andi McNair

Routledge
Taylor & Francis Group

NEW YORK AND LONDON

Designed cover image: © Getty Images

First published 2023
by Routledge
605 Third Avenue, New York, NY 10158

and by Routledge
4 Park Square, Milton Park, Abingdon, Oxon, OX14 4RN

Routledge is an imprint of the Taylor & Francis Group, an informa business

Library of Congress Cataloging-in-Publication Data
Names: McNair, Andi, 1977- author.
Title: Designing for depth in the classroom: a framework for purposeful differentiation/Andi McNair.
Description: New York, NY: Routledge, 2023. |
Includes bibliographical references. |
Identifiers: LCCN 2022031127 (print) | LCCN 2022031128 (ebook) |
ISBN 9781032393810 (hardback) | ISBN 9781032393780 (paperback) |
ISBN 9781003349471 (ebook)
Subjects: LCSH: Gifted children–Education. | Student-centered learning. |
Project method in teaching. | Motivation in education.
Classification: LCC LC3993 .M42 2023 (print) | LCC LC3993 (ebook) |
DDC 371.95–dc23/eng/20220914
LC record available at https://lccn.loc.gov/2022031127
LC ebook record available at https://lccn.loc.gov/2022031128

ISBN: 978-1-032-39381-0 (hbk)
ISBN: 978-1-032-39378-0 (pbk)
ISBN: 978-1-003-34947-1 (ebk)

DOI: 10.4324/9781003349471

Typeset in Palatino
by Deanta Global Publishing Services, Chennai, India

Dedicated to my husband, John, whose patience and support give me the time and space that I need to write, and to my children, Cory, Eli, and Katy, whose love and experience inspire me to keep advocating for sustainable change.

Table of Contents

Acknowledgments ix

Section I   **Moving Beyond the Shore**

Chapter 1   Introduction 3

Chapter 2   Intentional Differentiation 13

Section II   **Getting on the Board**

Chapter 3   Meaningful and Manageable 27

Chapter 4   Authentic Engagement.. 41

Section III   **Riding the Wave**

Chapter 5   Designing the Experience 59

Chapter 6   Beyond the Classroom Walls...................................... 73

Chapter 7   Knowing What They Need.. 83

Section IV   **Creating Soul Surfers**

Chapter 8   Providing Depth through Extension............................ 99

TABLE OF CONTENTS

Chapter 9   Providing Extra Support through Encouragement......127

Chapter 10   Creating the Perfect Wave 141

Meet the Author 151

Acknowledgments

My Savior—thankful that He sees me and provides purpose and perspective to guide the work.

My husband, John—thank you for supporting me through every project and making me feel as if I can change the world. I love you!

My kids, Cory, Eli, and Katy—thank you for your perspective and your willingness to always answer my questions about what you wish school could be. I love you guys more than you will ever know!

My parents, Ronnie and Ann Richardson—thank you for raising me in a home that made me believe that I could do anything that I set out to do. I am who I am today because of your willingness to encourage us and support us through our educational careers.

My sister, Mandi Killough—thanks for listening to me and always being my best friend. I'm glad that you are my sister!

Kari Espin—your thought partnership always pushes me to think way beyond what I think I'm capable of. Thank you for always listening, sharing ideas, and helping me grow.

Jaime Donally—thank you for being there to answer the hard questions and have the deep conversations. I'm so thankful for our friendship.

My Region 12 family—thank you for your support and encouragement. I learn so much from you all every day and I'm thankful to be a part of the work.

Section I

Moving Beyond the Shore

Chapter 1

Introduction

BIG IDEA

Learning, like surfing, should result in our learners being fully immersed in the experience as they are engaged, challenged, and given the opportunity to be better than they were the day before.

DOI: 10.4324/9781003349471-2

3

Have you ever really watched someone surf? I mean, really paid attention to their position and intentionality as they ride the waves? If you haven't, do me a favor and watch a couple of YouTube videos of people on their surfboards and pay attention. What do you notice?

You will probably notice the intensity of their focus and their full immersion in the experience. You see, surfers understand that in order to reach their goal of staying on the board and riding the perfect wave, they have to be actively engaged in the experience. They have to not only zone in on the wave that they are riding at the moment, but also be ready for the waves that are coming their way. They have to be willing to fully invest. Without a willingness to fully engage, a surfer will lose their focus and balance and end up wiping out.

At its core, engagement is a willingness to invest. I think that we, too often, settle for passivity and compliance in the classroom. You never see a surfer on the board with their hands by their sides, knees locked, and eyes straight ahead. That would be a passive approach to an experience that requires action. It simply wouldn't result in the outcome that most surfers are looking for, a thrilling opportunity to ride the waves and experience that adrenaline rush that they are seeking the moment they set out on their boards.

Instead, when you watch a surfer prepare to ride the waves, they take a moment to assess the current situation and grab their boards. They are excited to get into the water and begin to paddle out into what they know will challenge and engage them in a way that will make them better. In watching videos of surfers before a big ride, they are so jazzed and so excited about what lies ahead. Then, it happens. It's time to stand up on the board and ride the waves that will push them to be better than they were the last time they were in the water. It's a high-risk, high-reward situation that many surfers live for.

As they begin to engage in the experience, they find their balance and begin to ride the waves. They are looking around, arms out, and their knees are bent...they are ready for anything and they fully expect the unexpected. You see, that's what keeps surfers coming back into the water. They know that the one thing that they can expect is to be challenged, pushed beyond what they thought they were capable of achieving, and an opportunity to be a better surfer than they were the day before.

What if learning looked like this? What if, instead of coming to school expecting to be disengaged and bored, our learners hopped on their surfboards and prepared to ride the wave? What if they knew that they could expect the same thing that surfers expect as they paddle out into the water...an experience that will challenge them, push them, and provide an opportunity to be better than they were before?

My Story

It's funny because there was a point in my career when I didn't think this type of learning was possible. I fell into believing that school was just something that every learner needed to experience in order to "get to" their real lives and what they wanted to do beyond the walls of the classroom. But, nothing could be further from the truth. Instead, our classrooms should be like the waters that I previously described. Our learners should come into the classroom with an active willingness to invest, knowing that they will be engaged, challenged, and encouraged to go beyond what they think they can do. They should be ready and willing to ride the waves that will provide an experience that they will not soon forget.

In order to get to a place that helped me understand what my learners deserved from their classroom experience, I needed a complete shift in mindset. That mindset shift happened for me when I went from teaching math and science in a general education classroom to a content-mastery type of experience, and then finally found my niche and passion in a gifted and talented classroom working with learners that were practically begging to be challenged and pushed beyond what they had always known school to be. As I began to realize that these learners deserved so much more than a sit-and-get-learning experience, my perspective began to change.

I also began to realize that not only did my learners deserve more than that as students, but I also deserved more than that as an educator. It became very evident that I had become complacent and comfortable with doing what I had always done. I had stopped prioritizing engagement and instead, I simply expected compliance. Because of this perspective, I had, frankly, lost my love for doing the work.

And then, all of a sudden it became clear that if I wanted them to get on their boards and be willing to ride the waves, I was going to have to be the first one in the water. I was going to have to begin to do things that challenged me as an educator and the first step was to become more intentional about what I designed and expected from my learners.

Important Connections

I remember that my first "wave" was using social media to connect with other educators beyond my district. While this might not seem like a huge step for some, it was a huge step for me. At the time, I did not use social media often and the very thought of connecting with someone that I didn't know well made me super nervous. I had never utilized Twitter before and suddenly found myself using the platform to connect with educators all over the world. I couldn't get enough. As often as I could, I would scroll through my feed looking for educators that were doing things in their classrooms that aligned with what I knew I wanted for my learners. I began to learn so much and I was consistently pushed to think beyond what I thought my classroom could and should be.

Shifting My Mindset

I also began to read. I specifically remember reading *Teach Like a Pirate* by Dave Burgess and *Pure Genius* by Don Wettrick. As I took in everything that these amazing educators were sharing, I began to understand that the bottom line was that I needed to shift from writing lesson plans to designing experiences. I needed to understand what that looked like and how doing so would impact the gifted learners that I was currently serving in the classroom.

One of the first things that I did was look up the words "activity" and "experience" in the dictionary. As most of my friends and colleagues will tell you, I believe that words matter. If I'm going to use a word, I want to know exactly what it means and whether or not it's conveying the message that I want to convey. When I found the definitions, I realized that an activity is something that a person or group does and an experience is something that leaves an impression. I began to think to myself, "Who cares if they do it?", especially if it's done out of compliance. Instead, I wanted the things that I did in my classroom to leave an impression.

As I began to make the shift from writing lesson plans to designing experiences, it became clear that challenging my learners and thinking differently about how they learned was going to need to be a priority. My gifted learners were so desperate for the opportunity to dive deeper into specific concepts and explore complex ideas as a part of their learning experience.

The reality is that they often spent their days paddling out into the waters, waiting for a big wave that never came. In doing so, they had become frustrated, disengaged, and even apathetic during the school day.

Through my own experience in the classroom, I realized how often we make surface-level learning the priority simply because of time or what we think our learners are capable of. We are fine with them paddling out on their boards because, well, that's safe. Instead of high risk, high reward, it's low risk, no reward. Imagine if a surfer paddled out into the water with great expectations only to realize that the waves never came. Sadly, they would paddle back towards the shore, pack up their things, and head home. Sound familiar?

Because of what school looks like and how we play the game, we tend to present material to our learners as a checklist of things that should be learned rather than a bigger picture with deeper concepts and ideas. What we should be considering is how we, as educators, can create the perfect wave that our learners will be super stoked to ride.

The Perfect Wave

From what I've been able to determine, in the surfing realm, the perfect wave is often formed when the swell and the shore collide as this accelerates the water and provides speed (SurferToday.com, n.d.). I think this is interesting because I happen to think that the perfect learning experience happens when the standard, idea, or concept that is being shared collides with what our learners experience beyond the walls of the classroom. Oftentimes, although not always, our gifted learners learn at an accelerated pace and are ready to explore independently rather than waiting for everyone else to catch up. We will talk about this later in the book, but it is definitely key to designing an experience that learners will be willing to invest in.

I often wonder what might happen if we began to give our learners the opportunity to experience learning at a level of depth that will result in real understanding rather than surface-level learning. What if instead of asking them to paddle out into the waters only to find that the perfect wave doesn't exist, we focused on creating the perfect waves and encouraged them to get up on their boards and hang ten?

At this point, you might totally agree with me, but you're probably wondering what this looks like and how you can implement this mindset in your own classroom. How do we, as educators, design for depth in a way that will help our learners make important connections and understand what is being learned? How can we encourage them to grab their boards and hit the waves...even after falling off? How can we do this in a way that is not only meaningful for our learners but also manageable for educators? So, let's go there. For the remainder of this book, we will discuss practical ways to create the perfect wave for your learners while making meaningful differentiation a priority.

Reflection Questions

1. Take some time to watch a video of a surfer on their board. What connections can you make between that experience and what learners experience in the classroom?

2. What parts of learning look most like the surfing experience to you?

3. What does "the perfect wave" look like for you? In other words, what has to happen for our learners to want to ride the wave?

What is your biggest takeaway from Chapter 1?

_____

_____

_____

What challenged or validated something that you already knew?

_____

_____

_____

Work Cited

SurferToday.com, Editor at. (n.d.). *What is the ideal wave for surfing?* Surfertoday. Retrieved August 10, 2022, from https://www.surfertoday.com/surfing/what-is-the-ideal-wave-for-surfing.

Chapter 2

Intentional Differentiation

BIG IDEA

Designing for depth requires us to be intentional about the differentiation that is provided for every learner in our classroom.

DOI: 10.4324/9781003349471-3

Oftentimes, when I ask teachers what word comes to mind when they hear "differentiation," they say "overwhelming." Just thinking about knowing what every learner needs and then designing experiences that will meet their specific needs feels… well, impossible. Many educators have told me that sometimes differentiation feels like a guessing game. In fact, sometimes, learners receive the same type of differentiation all year long. In other words, if they are gifted, they always receive an extension. If they are a struggling learner, it is always assumed that they will need extra support.

I think one way that can we move beyond this feeling of being overwhelmed by the idea of differentiation is to focus on intentionality and consider every learner on the front end of designing a learning experience. Deliberate design will always result in a much more purposeful experience for both the educator and their learners. Let's take some time in this chapter to consider exactly what that looks like and why it's so important.

Flexible Grouping

If we really take the time to think through the way that we often group our learners, it simply doesn't make sense. We all have things that we understand and things that we don't. Therefore, flexible grouping should be a priority in every classroom.

Carol Ann Tomlinson describes this type of grouping as "a consistent flow of varied student groupings within a unit of study based on the nature of the work and the individual needs of students" (Tomlinson & Imbeau, 2010, p. 90). This is the only type of grouping that makes sense in my mind. The key words are "the individual needs of students." Our learners all bring different thoughts, experiences, strengths, and weaknesses to the table. The issue is that those same words are the words that make differentiation seem overwhelming.

In this chapter, I hope to share how to see differentiation from a perspective that will make sense and seem more manageable. It's no secret that we sometimes make things harder than they actually are within the education community and I think differentiation is a perfect example of that reality in many classrooms.

Designing for Depth

Designing for depth...it's a different way to plan. In fact, it's a different way to design. First, let's just think about the shift from planning to designing. One of the definitions of design is to "do or plan (something) with a specific purpose or intention in mind." Intentionality is key when it comes to designing experiences and will always result in a bigger return on our investment as educators. When I look back on my early years in the classroom and consider what was missing, intentionality comes to mind. I often did things because I was supposed to or because it was what the curriculum suggested. I rarely took the time to consider why I was doing it and what I hoped the outcome would be.

As educators, we do so much more than simply plan lessons. When I hear an educator say how much they hate lesson planning, I can't help but wonder how much more they would love designing experiences. There's a difference, and in my opinion, one of the main differences is that when you are designing experiences, intentionality is prioritized. Ultimately, our goal should be that whatever we design and whatever our learners experience in our classroom leave an impression on them. Because, if it doesn't...what's the point?

Surface-Level Learning vs. Deep Understanding

Surface-Level Learning

I do think that there is a difference between learning and understanding. While both are important, it's imperative to consider the difference and recognize which outcome will be achieved through what is being done in the classroom. I have often asked educators to look at an experience that has been designed and label the different parts of that experience SL (surface level) and DU (deep understanding). Then, I ask them to consider the ratio of surface-level learning to the opportunities to reach deep understanding. This experience can result in clarity and a realization of what is being prioritized and how it is impacting learning in the classroom.

So often, gifted learners already have a surface-level understanding of what is being introduced. They are even able to demonstrate that surface-level understanding in a way that leads to many educators assuming that they are ready to move on to something new. Instead of mistaking surface-level learning as a readiness to move on to an entirely different concept, it's important that we consider that they often need the opportunity to go beyond the surface level in order to deeply understand the concept or standard.

Deep Understanding

You might be asking yourself what "deep understanding" looks like. What makes deep understanding different from surface-level learning? I might be guilty of oversimplifying this, but I believe that deep understanding is evident when a learner can apply what has been learned in a variety of ways, when they can use what they've learned to design something new or share what they know with someone else. This is why any type of project-based learning can be so meaningful and have such an impact. We will explore project-based learning in a later chapter, but it's important to mention that as far as deep understanding goes, project-based learning is the most authentic and sensible answer. It gives learners an opportunity to apply, design, create, and make connections.

Level 4 of Webb's Depth of Knowledge is Extended Thinking, and many resources share that this level requires learners to address authentic problems through investigation (Hammer, 2018). We will explore this resource and framework a little later in the book but it makes sense that learners are always going to be more engaged when they can connect what is being learned to something that they are interested in or familiar with beyond the walls of the classroom. Connections play a big role in the classroom and can result in real learning when they are utilized to ignite a willingness to invest.

Creating Set Waves for Gifted Learners

In writing this book, I have done lots of research on surfing and surfers. In doing so, I learned that set waves are waves that come in groups of two or more. These are the waves the surfers seek out because they offer more power and longer rides ("Speak Like a Surfer? 40 Surfing Terms and Phrases You Should Know"). While not every surfer is ready to ride a set wave, those that are might become bored when riding small whitewater waves, the easiest waves to ride.

The same is true for a gifted learner or any learner that already understands a concept, idea, or standard that is being introduced in the classroom. They are fully aware that the opportunity exists to catch a longer, more powerful wave. You can imagine how frustrating this can be and how if the opportunity to catch that set wave never comes, they will eventually give up and hang up their board.

Encouraging our learners to be willing to explore beyond their comfort zones is not an easy task. It can be scary to experience learning at a depth that could result in struggle or even failure. Think about how intimidating it must be to go out into the ocean to experience bigger waves than you've ever experienced before. However, we know that sometimes, it's through those experiences that the best learning happens.

In fact, without the willingness to tackle the "big waves," a surfer will never become the soul surfer that many of them set out to be. In one of the chapters to come, we will discuss the idea of productive struggle and how we can make it part of our classroom culture and help our learners value it as part of the learning process.

Gifted learners sit in our classrooms every single day and many of them experience a traditional learning experience that simply does not make sense for who they are as learners. In other words, they are bored, disengaged, and can even become apathetic as a result of already knowing what is being shared or finishing their work before the rest of the class.

While most of us, as educators, know this and would like to provide a solution, it just seems overwhelming to meet the needs of our learners who understand while we are most concerned about the learners that don't. It's easier to give our gifted learners and high achievers a project or busywork (yes, I went there) than to intentionally consider what they can do when they finish early or announce that they already understand.

Designing for Depth

Jamie O'Brien, a professional surfer, once said that "There is no one right way to ride a wave" (SurferToday.com, n.d.). The same is true for learning in the classroom and designing the experiences for the learners that come into our classrooms every single day. Our learners will approach waves differently, and as educators, we will approach designing experiences differently.

In my experience, differentiation is not as difficult as we sometimes think it is. Instead, I think that with a little intentionality and a toolbox of strategies and ideas, we can frontload what learners that understand will experience as extension or enrichment and what learners that don't understand will experience as extra support. And, instead of it being completely disconnected from what is being learned by the rest of the class, it should simply be an opportunity to go deeper, explore independently, or think differently about the content.

I remember how overwhelmed I felt by differentiation early in my career. If only I had known and understood what I know and understand now, I would have approached this aspect of teaching from a completely different perspective.

As I've shared, designing for depth requires us to consider every learner on the front end of a learning experience rather than the back end. When I think back to how I differentiated for gifted learners early on in my career, I cringe a little. To be honest, I didn't even consider giving them something different until they had already finished early or shared that they already understood what was being learned. This resulted in me providing busywork or a meaningless extension worksheet rather than a meaningful learning experience that would give them the opportunity to dive deeper and reach a deeper understanding of what was being learned.

After being given the opportunity to teach in a gifted education classroom, I began to recognize that if we designed experiences with these learners in mind, we would be creating a much more meaningful experience for them and a much more manageable experience for us. It makes so much more sense to design for depth rather than to plan for compliance.

So, why should we design for depth? Because the reality is that this perspective is what will give us the opportunity to meet the needs of all of our learners. It will provide a framework for intentionality and help us create meaningful experiences that will leave an impression on our learners. In the following chapters, we will talk about how to not only design for depth, but also utilize specific ideas, strategies, and tools that already exist to accomplish many of the things that I've shared so far. I'm excited to help you understand how this can be done in a way that is both manageable and meaningful. I'm also excited about sharing how meeting the needs of gifted learners is not as difficult as we sometimes assume. It simply requires us to be intentional and purposeful as we design experiences from a different perspective.

A Gifted Learner's Perspective

I talk with gifted learners often as part of the work that I do and one of their biggest frustrations is being given busywork or being asked to run errands because they have already finished the work that the rest of the class is doing or have already demonstrated understanding. They also struggle with the fact that they are sometimes asked to do work at a level that they have already mastered. It's as if we are asking them to play a level of a video game again even though they have made it through that level and are ready to level up. It doesn't make sense.

Gifted learners become very frustrated with having to play a game that was designed for a specific type of learner. When we recognize that they learn differently or think in different ways, we often create unrealistic expectations by providing more work or harder work rather than providing more meaningful work. Because of these frustrations, gifted learners can sometimes begin to act out or completely disengage from the school experience. In order to keep this from happening, it's important that we consider how we can ignite an active willingness to invest from them, as well as the rest of our learners.

Autonomy and Independence

Consider this: if you knew how to surf the most difficult of waves but you were with a group of surfers that were just learning how to get on their boards, how might you feel? While they were nervous about getting in the water and excited about learning the basics, you would know and understand that you were capable of paddling out into the water and riding the waves. Your experience would be so much more appropriate and engaging if you were given the opportunity to go beyond the shoreline. Instead of focusing on what was being shared or experienced, you would probably be thinking about all of the things that you could be doing and seeing if you were only given the autonomy and independence to do so.

Autonomy and independence can be scary and I'm speaking from experience. When I changed my perspective in my classroom from teacher-driven to learner-driven, I was scared to death. I had no idea how they would respond or how they might handle the responsibility. And, to be honest, they didn't handle it well in the beginning. While many of my learners needed and deserved the opportunity to go deeper, they were so used to simply paddling beyond the shoreline that they weren't sure how to even stand up on the board without me there telling them exactly how to do so. They didn't have the self-awareness or self-management skills that they needed to stay focused or guide their own learning.

I always want to be transparent about my experience. It was difficult to help my learners get to a place where they felt comfortable learning and discovering without someone telling them how, what, when, and where to do their work. However, difficult doesn't mean impossible and through lots of conversation, scaffolding, and honestly, just letting go, we were able to get to a place that we've talked about earlier in this book—a place where the learning experiences that I designed were manageable for me and meaningful for them.

Reflection Questions

1. What do you think the difference is between surface-level learning and deep understanding?

2. What roles do autonomy and independence currently play in your classroom?

3. On a scale of 1–5, how much of a priority has differentiating for gifted learners and high achievers been in your classroom?

What is your biggest takeaway from Chapter 2?

_____

_____

_____

What challenged or validated something that you already knew?

_____

_____

_____

Works Cited

Hammer, B. (2018, August). *Webb's depth of knowledge framework: The basics*. Edmentum.com. Retrieved from blog.edmentum.com/webb%E2%80%99s-depth-knowledge-framework-basics.

The best surfing quotes of all time. (n.d.). Surfertoday. Surfertoday. Retrieved from www.surfertoday.com/surfing/the-best-surfing-quotes-of-all-time.

Tomlinson, C.A., & Imbeau, M.D. (2011) *Leading and managing a differentiated classroom*. Hawker Brownlow Education.

Section II

Getting on the Board

Chapter 3

Meaningful and Manageable

BIG IDEA

If what educators are implementing or being asked to implement in the classroom isn't both manageable and meaningful, the reality is that it will not be sustainable.

DOI: 10.4324/9781003349471-5

Over the last few years, I've had the opportunity to see and experience a variety of lesson planning templates. And I'll be honest…it's very rare that I see a template that requires educators to intentionally plan for extension or enrichment. There is often an opportunity to consider what will be done for those that don't understand, but not those that do. And that's not okay.

You see, if we honestly want to meet the needs of every learner, we have to design with every learner in mind. So, over the last couple of years, I've been working on a framework. I've considered what this should look like and how we can make this a priority without feeling completely overwhelmed. I've looked at a variety of templates and considered what would really allow us to create that perfect wave that I talked about in Chapter 1.

I've seen some great examples and some terrible examples. I've seen templates that simply did not consider manageability and templates that did not consider the meaningfulness of the experiences for our learners. After all of this, I decided to create a framework that I thought would result in a meaningful learning experience designed to meet the needs of every learner.

So, we've talked about why it's important to design for depth. The next question becomes, "How do you design for depth?" The rest of this book will provide practical ideas and resources to make designing for depth something that you can implement immediately into your own classroom.

As we talked about in Chapter 2, one of the things that I hear most often about differentiation is that it is difficult to manage. It's overwhelming and can often seem like one more thing that we are adding to the extremely loaded plates that teachers already carry.

In the pages to come, I want to introduce this framework for designing for depth which I think provides the intentionality that is so important when designing an experience. But before I do that, I want to share my thoughts about considerations that have to be made before implementing new ideas and new strategies into any classroom.

Two Important Questions

I remember so many times when I was in the classroom being asked to implement something that was introduced into our district. I remember sitting through professional learning experiences that involved a speaker introducing a new idea or concept that they were trying to persuade us to implement in our classrooms. When I found myself in these situations, I often found myself feeling as if there just wasn't room on my plate to add anything new. I would become frustrated and would often disengage out of the realization that I just wasn't going to be able to make it happen…regardless of how great of an idea it was.

Now that I am able to reflect on that experience, I am able to recognize that I just wasn't asking the right questions. Instead of taking the time to purposefully consider what was being shared, I just made the assumption that it was too much and that I didn't have time. And, there were times that I either had to implement something out of compliance, or I decided to implement it because it sounded like the magic bullet…FYI, that doesn't exist. In doing so, I would make it work for a short amount of time and then it would often fizzle out because I hadn't really thought through how to make it sustainable.

After lots of conversations with teachers and reflecting on my own experience, I've realized that in order for anything to be sustainable, it has to be manageable for educators and meaningful for their learners. Otherwise, there is no reason to continue to invest in the idea or the process because the reality is that it will not be sustainable.

In this chapter, we will explore these two questions as a framework for making the aspect of designing for depth sustainable in any classroom. These two questions are extremely important for educational leaders to consider before introducing a new idea, strategy, or even a new tool for teachers to implement. But they are also important for us, as educators, to consider when we are asked to do something different in our classrooms.

1. Is it manageable?
2. Is it meaningful?

And here's the thing…if the answer is no to either of those questions, that doesn't mean that it can't be done. It simply means that we must ask ourselves, "How do we make it so?" If what we are asking educators to do isn't manageable, what can be done so that it is? And, then, we must ask the same question on behalf of our learners. If it isn't meaningful for our learners, how can we make it so?

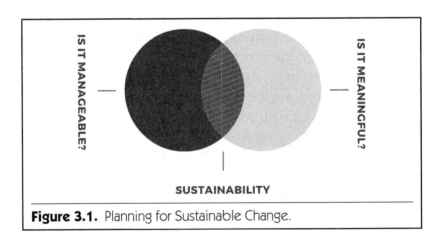

Figure 3.1. Planning for Sustainable Change.

I strongly believe that, as a system, we sometimes lose focus and forget to ask the questions that need to be asked when we are encouraging educators to try something new in the class-room. When we make the decision to be proactive, everything changes. But the reality is that we are all too often reactive. We learn about something new and shiny that we would like to see implemented and roll it out without careful consideration or thinking about the user experience.

So, before implementing anything that is shared in this book, from a professional learning experience, or from someone in your district, ask yourself, "How will I make this meaningful for my learners?" and "How will I make this manageable for me?" Doing so will result in a more sustainable approach and will help you take a much more realistic approach to what is and isn't implemented in your classroom, on your campus, or in your district.

Now that you understand what the two questions are and why they are so important to ask before implementation, let's dive deeper into each one and consider how we can make this happen from a practical perspective.

Making It Meaningful

As I shared at the beginning of this chapter, when considering new strategies and ideas, the first consideration should be, "Is this meaningful for my learners?" I've said it before and I'll say it again, if what we're teaching in the classroom isn't meaningful for our learners, it's a waste of our time and theirs. Determining whether or not something will be meaningful requires us to understand who our learners are and what they need from a learning experience.

This is not always easy to do, but if we aren't willing to know them well, how will we know what is and isn't meaningful for them? Taking the time to ask them questions about what they enjoy or listening to them talk with their friends about their experiences beyond the walls of the classroom can give us valuable information that can be used to help them make important connections.

Differentiation is a way for us to make learning more meaningful for every learner. Without making differentiation a priority, what is being learned will not be meaningful to our learners as individuals. The learning might feel too small or too big. A one-size-fits-all approach is like expecting a group of people to all wear the same size of blue jeans...not going to happen. Too often, we design experiences with a limited reach. And, then we are frustrated when do not get the expected return on our investment. Instead, it feels as if we are spinning our wheels and not making any progress. Without considering what our learners need after a learning experience, the experience might be appropriate for one or two groups of learners, but the reality is that it will not be meaningful for all.

Consider gifted learners that often already know what is being taught in the classroom on any given day. We all know what it feels like to sit through something that either a) you already know and understand or b) doesn't concern you in any way. I don't know about you, but when I'm in these situations, I feel super frustrated and unseen. I have a feeling that gifted learners often feel the same way. This is why it's really important that we give careful consideration to how meaningful a learning experience will be before we implement it in our classrooms.

In my book, *A Meaningful Mess: A Teacher's Guide to Student-Driven Classrooms, Authentic Learning, Student Empowerment, and Keeping It All Together Without Losing Your Mind*, I shared three questions to consider when deciding whether or not technology should be implemented in the classroom (McNair, 2019). After writing that book, I quickly realized that those same three questions should be considered when deciding if anything is meaningful enough to be implemented in the classroom.

1. Will it engage and empower my learners?
2. Will it help my learners make connections?
3. Will it deepen their understanding?

When designing a learning experience, these questions are really important. Let's be honest, if they aren't engaged, they will not be invested. Without connections, the learning will not be meaningful, and if it doesn't deepen their understanding, we are simply expecting surface-level learning that will not stick.

It's important that we recognize that it doesn't matter whether or not what we are sharing is meaningful for us; it matters if it's meaningful for them. This can be difficult. Even if we know it's meaningful or will be meaningful for them at some point, if we can't help them understand how it's meaningful and relevant right now, it will be difficult for them to make the connection.

Let's look at this idea through an analogy. Imagine yourself at the grocery store and someone comes up to you in aisle eight and starts putting random things in your basket. How would you react? You would probably become quickly frustrated and ask, "What in the world are you doing?" I would suspect that you would even start returning the things that they were putting in your basket back to the shelf. Isn't that what it feels like, sometimes, in the classroom? It feels as if we are putting things in their basket and they are putting it right back on the shelf.

Now, let's look at this from a different perspective. What if, instead of just putting random things in your basket, the person was explaining that they were putting them in your basket for a specific reason? What if they said, "Andi, I'm putting sugar in your basket because your husband loves sweet tea and you are almost out," or "I'm putting pancake syrup in your basket because you are feeding the football team on Friday morning and you don't have any syrup for the pancakes." We would all probably react very differently to that situation. We would be appreciative and thankful and might even ask if we could do this more often.

The only difference between those two situations is the why. There was a reason that the things were being put in my basket and knowing that reason made the experience more meaningful. The same is true in the classroom. If our learners not only know what we are putting in their baskets but also understand why, the learning will be more meaningful and they will likely be more willing to invest.

Making It Manageable

The second question that, honestly, is not being asked enough right now in education is, "Is this manageable for me or for the educator who will be implementing the idea?" There are so many ideas, concepts, and strategies that seem like great ideas and may even be meaningful for our learners, but they simply aren't manageable. In other words, the implementation of what is being expected or considered hasn't been a priority. This happens often and will always result in frustration and an unwillingness to invest from the educator's perspective.

I want to be clear and share that I do not believe that we should refuse to implement something simply because it isn't manageable. However, as I shared earlier, I believe that it is important that we are given the opportunity to ask, "How do we make it so?" There is absolutely nothing wrong with telling an administrator, colleague, or the person asking you to implement a specific idea or strategy that it doesn't feel manageable and you would like feedback or ideas to implement so that it will be.

Let's take Genius Hour for example. Genius Hour or passion-based learning involves giving learners an opportunity to pursue their passions and/or interests during the school day. In doing so, they are encouraged to make an impact or create change. This type of learning provides a big return on investment for educators as learners are given the opportunity to learn by doing while exploring something that is meaningful to them. As you may know, passion-based learning is the one thing in my classroom that changed everything. Giving my learners the opportunity to use what they loved to change something that bothered them created a learning environment that I had no idea existed.

However, when I first started to implement this strategy in my own classroom, it was a mess! I was overwhelmed, my learners were overwhelmed, and it quickly became too much for any of us to handle. While it was easy for me to realize how meaningful this type of learning experience was for them, I knew that I was going to need to consider how to make Genius Hour more manageable for me.

So, I began to look at what other educators were doing and I began to consider what made it feel as if it wasn't manageable. In doing so, I realized that my learners needed a process, a roadmap, if you will, for this experience. I knew that if we had a process for them to follow, there would be some level of consistency and an opportunity for me to streamline the parts of the projects that were just too much for one educator to handle. After a great deal of thought and consideration, the Six Ps of Genius Hour (McNair, 2017) were born and we never looked back.

That experience is the perfect example of being honest about your current reality. I knew it wasn't manageable and I knew it wasn't going to continue to work in the way that we initially thought that it would. So, we pivoted. I chose to consider the small tweaks that could be made to make it as manageable for me as it was meaningful for them.

The reality is that manageability is really important to consider before implementing or asking teachers to implement something in the classroom because when it's not manageable, it will be difficult to continue doing it for any amount of time. So, let's talk about what manageability looks like. How do we know if what we are being asked to implement will be manageable for us, as educators? After thinking through this, considering my experience with Genius Hour, and talking to other educators, these are the questions that I think will bring clarity.

1. Is it doable?
2. Can it be done without great difficulty or added stress?
3. Can it continue to be done over time?

First of all, manageable does not mean easy, in my opinion. Instead, it means doable. There is a difference. Asking ourselves if something is doable requires us to be honest about what is on our plate. If the answer is no, we have to ask why that's the case. Is it not doable because we don't have the tools or resources? Is it not doable because we don't have the ability? Or is not doable because there are simply too many other things on our plate?

There are so many things that educators are expected to do that cause stress simply because they are made more difficult than they need to be. Differentiation is a perfect example of this. When done well and with intention, this should not be difficult enough to add a great deal of stress. In fact, it might even make the classroom more manageable, as your learners will be actively engaged and more willing to invest.

Educators become frustrated when it feels as if what they are being asked to do isn't going to be sustainable. If something isn't going to be able to be implemented over time, it's difficult to see a reason to make it a priority in the first place. However, when something seems manageable, it seems sustainable, and sustainability is a key characteristic when considering whether or not something is going to be implemented.

These two concepts—meaningfulness and manageability—are so important because the reality is that without them, there is no sustainability. It begins to feel as if we are just throwing eggs against a wall. Then, we slowly watch them slide down that wall until they no longer exist and we throw more eggs. The only way to make the egg stick to the wall is to consider the possibilities before you let go of the egg. Trying to keep it on the wall after it's been thrown is futile because it is a reactive approach.

Reflection Questions

1. Have you ever tried to implement something that wasn't meaningful for your learners? What was the outcome?

2. Have you ever been asked to implement something that wasn't manageable for you? What was the outcome?

3. How do you think that considering these two questions might benefit you as an educator? How might it benefit your learners?

What is your biggest takeaway from Chapter 3?

_____
_____
_____

What challenged or validated something that you already knew?

_____
_____
_____

Works Cited

McNair, A. (2019). *A meaningful mess: A teacher's guide to student-driven classrooms, authentic learning, student empowerment, and keeping it all together without losing your mind.* Prufrock Press Inc.

McNair, A. (2017). *Genius hour: Passion projects that ignite innovation and student inquiry.* Prufrock Press Inc.

Chapter 4

Authentic
Engagement

BIG IDEA

If we don't take the time to engage, or ignite an active willingness to invest in today's learners, it will be extremely difficult to provide the opportunity to learn.

DOI: 10.4324/9781003349471-6

Engagement…this is possibly one of the most utilized words when it comes to describing what educators do in the classroom. However, I sometimes feel that the over-usage of this word has led to it being less of a priority. We all know how quickly a word can become a buzzword in the educational community. And once that happens, that word becomes more and more difficult to hear and can even begin to lose its power. I'm not suggesting that, as educators, we don't all want to engage our learners. I know that for most of those that are in the classroom, that is the goal each and every day.

However, as we discussed earlier in the book, intentionality is key. Engagement will not just happen and honestly, it probably won't be easy. Engaging today's learners requires us to really consider who they are and what they need from the learning experiences that we design. At its core, engagement is an active willingness to invest. It's the spark that makes the fire possible and if we fail to light that spark, the fire will not burn.

Life-Ready and Social-Emotional Learning Skills

One of the key ways to engage today's learners is through authenticity. Simply learning content isn't enough for them because they have access to content in their pockets. That doesn't mean that they don't need to learn the content, it just means that we must consider more than that as we are designing an experience.

When the learning feels authentic, it feels natural to engage. When the learning feels forced and foreign, they will almost always disengage. So, how do we do that? How do we make learning authentic and feel as if it is about more than just the content? Let's talk about it.

If it's important to understand that designing for depth requires us to think beyond the content and standards that are being learned, what does that look like? When designing for depth, it's also important to consider what the ideas, concepts, and standards that are being learned will look like beyond the walls of the classroom. We can make this happen by weaving life-ready and social-emotional learning skills into the learning experiences that we design.

I think, as educators, we often make the mistake of feeling as though we should only teach these concepts or skills in isolation. In other words, the counselor will come in on Thursday to provide a social-emotional learning experience with our students and we check off that box. We often don't get around to making life-ready skills like collaboration, creativity, communication, critical thinking, reflection, and kindness, or the social-emotional skills like self-awareness, self-management, social awareness, relationships skills, and decision-making skills ("CASEL–CASEL") a priority, simply because there isn't time to add anything else to the plate.

Instead of thinking of these skills being an entirely different dish, it's a better idea to see them as the seasoning that we sprinkle on top of the dish to make it taste better. In other words, I don't think that these skills should simply be taught in isolation. Instead, intentionally weaving them into the experiences that we design will make the experience more authentic and learners will be more likely to invest. While modeling these skills and explicitly introducing them is a good idea, it's the feedback regarding these skills that will have the biggest impact on our learners. And if we are designing for depth, this isn't difficult to achieve.

When designing a learning experience, we have to consider these skills. I tend to look back at the experience after it's been designed to consider where these skills can be woven in. When can I give my learners the opportunity to collaborate? What decisions can I allow them to make? Have I given them the opportunity to think critically about what is being learned? You get the idea.

You might be able to weave in three life-ready and social-emotional learning skills or you may be able to weave in two. The point is that we are intentional about weaving them in and providing feedback on how our learners utilize these skills to accomplish whatever it is that they have been tasked with completing.

Engage: a Key Piece of the Learning Experience

In my work with both educators and today's learners, I've realized that there are specific parts of a learning experience that simply cannot be excluded. In addition to weaving in both life-ready and social-emotional learning skills, we must consider how to ignite a willingness to invest as soon as our learners walk into the classroom. How can we engage them before providing the opportunity to learn? Because the reality is that without a willingness to invest, it's difficult to provide the opportunity to learn.

Look, this is not a new idea. Many of you know this as a hook or an anticipatory set. Whatever you call it, it's the prioritization of engaging your learners through intentionally igniting a willingness to invest before doing anything else.

Why Prioritize Engagement?

I do not believe that the engaging piece of a learning experience always has to be directly connected to what is being learned that day. Let me explain what I mean by this. I was recently sharing this idea with a group of educators in a local district. I could tell that one of the educators disagreed with this comment or was, at the very least, giving it careful consideration. After the presentation, he came to chat with me and shared that he wasn't sure whether or not he agreed with the fact that the hook didn't need to explicitly connect with what was being learned that day.

However, after thinking through it, he made an important connection. He said that he was the song leader at his church and when they warmed up before the service, they didn't sing the same songs that they were going to sing in the service that day. He shared that they utilized that time to get their voices ready and prepared for the service itself. And, I responded with, "*Yes!* That's exactly my point." The goal is to prepare their minds and ignite a willingness to invest. If what you do in the first five or ten minutes of class accomplishes that, then you will be building the foundation for a great day of learning.

It's important to engage your learners as soon as they walk in the door. In other words, even if you need to do attendance or talk to a teacher next door, there should be something for them to talk about in groups or respond to independently. This might be hard to hear, but a bell ringer worksheet is not what I'm talking about. I won't say never, but I will say that a worksheet will rarely jazz your learners up for the learning experience that lies ahead.

Utilizing Curiosity to Engage

A great place to start when looking for ways to engage your learners is the Eight Cs of Engagement. These were created and developed by Harvey F. Silver and Matthew J. Perini (2010). They include competition, cooperation, creativity, challenge, choice, curiosity, connections, and controversy. I love utilizing these as a resource because it makes it easy to choose one as a way to start class each day. So often, we talk about how important engagement is, but we don't talk about how to make it happen. The Eight Cs of Engagement give educators practical ideas that can be implemented immediately into the classroom.

As you are designing an experience and determining what you will have your learners do as soon as they walk into class, consider one of the Eight Cs of Engagement. Will you engage them through a critical thinking challenge, will you help them make a connection to the content through a pop culture reference, or maybe even ignite their curiosity by asking them to make a prediction about what they will learn?

All of the Eight Cs of Engagement are effective ways to ignite a willingness to invest. However, I want to spend a little bit of time in this chapter exploring curiosity. When I talk to educators, one of the things that I hear most often is that today's learners simply aren't curious. Instead, they expect to be spoon-fed and aren't willing to ask questions and seek additional information. I believe that this is a result of the way that they experience learning when they come to school. Curiosity has to be cultivated. It has to be developed and then nurtured.

One of my favorite ways to engage learners through curiosity is through prediction. I recently read an article on the Mindshift blog entitled "How to Create Deeper Student Learning Experiences Through Authentic Questions" (Peeples, 2022). In that article, Shanna Peeples shares an excerpt from her book, *Think Like Socrates: Using Questions to Invite Wonder and Empathy Into the Classroom, Grades 4–12* (2019). My favorite part of this excerpt is that Peeples shares Judy Willis's perspective when it comes to curiosity. Willis is a neurologist and middle-school teacher and she explains that,

> Students' curiosity, along with their written or verbal predictions, will tune their brains into the perfect zone for attentive focus. They are like adults placing bets on a horse race. Students may not be interested in the subject matter itself, but their brains need to find out if their predictions are correct, just as the race ticket holder needs to know if he holds a winning ticket.
>
> (Willis, 2014)

That makes so much sense, doesn't it?

I oftentimes will determine the accuracy of an analogy by putting myself in the situation that is being utilized to make the point. So, when I read this quote, I asked myself how I might react if my husband and I were at a horse race and I had made a prediction regarding which horse was going to win. Then, I thought about how I might react if, after making that prediction, my husband wanted to leave the race before the horses ran. And I realized that I wouldn't want to leave. Even though I am not a fan of horse racing, I would want to stay at the race just to see if my prediction was correct. Wouldn't you?

So, now that we've established the power of prediction, let's talk about a couple of practical ways to make it happen in the classroom. I'm a big fan of images and think that most learners are, too. Pictures can often be more powerful than words and using them in the classroom to engage learners at the beginning of a learning experience makes perfect sense.

One of my favorite strategies is to have an image or even a GIF or meme projected as learners walk into the classroom. This works best if the image is not directly related to the content that will be shared that day. Let me give you an example.

Oftentimes, when I'm sharing this strategy with educators, I will model it by sharing the image of a grasshopper. I will ask them to think about the content that they teach and try to make a connection. It always takes a few minutes, but then all of a sudden, the responses start coming.

Most people wouldn't think about math when they see the image of a grasshopper. However, through this experience, many often recognize that the grasshopper's legs represent different types of angles, measurement can be used to determine how far a grasshopper might jump, and elapsed time can be used to explain the life cycle of a grasshopper. And then everyone in the room realizes that making the connections, another one of the Eight Cs of Engagement, simply requires us to think critically and beyond what is typically expected in the classroom. And, let's be honest, this is easy. It requires very little prep work but will give you a big return on your investment.

Curiosity can also be cultivated by encouraging our learners to ask questions. When they walk into class, expecting to be spoon-fed, they do not think about the questions that they should be asking. I love the idea of utilizing the Question Formulation Technique from the Right Question Institute (Right Question Institute, 2018). This technique encourages learners to produce and prioritize questions that they have about a specific idea or topic.

In a nutshell, teachers give learners a focus topic. Next, they encourage their learners to work in groups to formulate as many questions as they can regarding that topic. This strategy is valuable for gifted learners as they often want to tell others what they already know rather than acknowledging what they don't.

Then, they work together to prioritize their questions. You can learn more about this strategy and exactly how to implement it at rightquestion.org.

Can you imagine how this might impact the rest of the learning experience? As you are providing the opportunity to learn, your students will make connections to the questions that they created. As described in the horse race analogy, they will be engaging in the experience because they will want to know if their question is going to be answered. It makes so much sense and just like utilizing an image at the beginning of class, this strategy is very manageable for educators and meaningful for their learners.

Five Levels of Engagement

Phillip Schlecty identified and created five levels of engagement that are important to consider in any classroom and I would be remiss if I didn't talk about them in this chapter (Schlechty, 2011). When I think about these levels as well as the learners that I had in my classroom every day, each of these levels was represented. I had learners that fit the description of every level on this spectrum.

In his work, Phillip Schlechty focuses on two things: attention and commitment. Just because a learner is paying attention doesn't mean that they are engaged...it might just mean that they are compliant.

One of my favorite quotes from Phillip Schlechty is, "The business of schools is to design, create, and invent high-quality, intellectually demanding schoolwork that students find engaging" (2011). I often ask myself if this is how I viewed lesson planning. Did I see it as an opportunity to "design high-quality, intellectually demanding" work for my learners or was I just going through the motions? I also like that he makes it clear in this statement that it's about what students find engaging. It doesn't matter how engaging we think it should be, it matters how engaging it is. Paying attention to where our learners fall within the levels that Schlechty has created can help with this determination.

Taking the time to really prioritize engagement enough to know where our learners are on the spectrum gives us a better opportunity to decide what needs to happen moving forward. Understanding how engaged our learners are is similar to triage in the hospital. Different levels of engagement require different degrees of urgency. While every learner deserves to be fully engaged, a learner that is completely disengaged, apathetic, and maybe even defiant can affect the rest of the learners in the classroom. Let's take some time to discuss and explore the five levels of engagement identified by Philip Schlechty and consider how we might use this information to ignite an active willingness to invest.

Rebellion: Diverted Attention, No Commitment

The complete opposite of engagement is rebellion. Rebellion is simply a complete lack of engagement and actual defiance on the part of the learner being asked to invest. Schlechty explains this as diverted attention and no commitment. These students are often the ones acting out and doing everything that they can to be a distraction and avoid what they are actually being asked to do. For gifted learners, this is often the case if they have become tired of playing the game.

They will often become defiant and rebel in order to avoid doing something that they already know how to do. The opposite may also be true. They might rebel or become a distraction because they do not know how to do something. Instead of everyone becoming aware of this reality, it's easier to act out or do anything in their power to avoid having to admit that there might be something that they don't understand.

Sometimes the gifted label makes a learner think that they should know everything and never experience struggle. As educators, most of us realize that there is nothing further from the truth. It's important to pay attention to why a student is being rebellious and it's even more important to recognize when it's appropriate to have a conversation and when it's appropriate to provide a consequence.

Retreatism: Low Attention, Low Commitment

Retreatism is the passive approach to learning that often looks like apathy and boredom. These are the learners that often underachieve and just seemingly don't want to be in our classrooms. Within the spectrum, retreatism is explained as no attention and no commitment.

Can you imagine a surfer on the board with their shoulders slumped, knees locked, and eyes straight ahead? That's a perfect example of what these learners often look like in class. They may be on the board, but there is absolutely no investment or effort on their part to be a part of the experience. They may not be disruptive, but they may neglect to complete the work that they are given, choose to opt out of classroom discussions, and just seem distant or distracted most of the time that they are in the classroom.

Ritual Compliance: Low Attention, Low Commitment

Ritual compliance is what I believe that we see most often in the classroom and this involves learners doing the bare minimum to get by or get credit for the work that they are being asked to do. I have seen this so often and I think it's most prevalent as students begin to get older and learn how to play the game. They quickly understand that if they come to school and comply, they will simply be spoon-fed the information and then given the opportunity to regurgitate that information on a worksheet or unit test. Because they are simply going through the motions, there is no real engagement here. In fact, ritual compliance is distinguished by low attention and low commitment.

Strategic Compliance: High Attention, Low Commitment

Strategic compliance is a bit more active and is often the result of learners investing because of extrinsic motivation. In other words, they've learned how to play the game. Let's be honest...extrinsic motivation is never a long-term solution. Sure, many of our gifted learners will work for and strive for a good grade, especially those learners that want to please their teachers and parents and earn recognition for a job well done. But is that really what we want them to think is important? I'm not suggesting that good grades aren't a positive experience, but I am suggesting that I would rather my learners be motivated by something that will be beneficial outside of the classroom.

Later in the book, we are going to explore the role that intrinsic motivation can play in a learning experience. I think that when we do, you will see how much more beneficial it is if we take the time to consider playing the long game rather than the short game. Strategic compliance is explained by Phillip Schlechty as high attention and low commitment.

Engagement: High Attention, High Commitment

Finally, true engagement involves learners being actively involved and self-driven. This pinnacle of what learning should look like in the classroom is described by high attention and high commitment. Intrinsic motivation is often the catalyst for this type of engagement. An engaged learner is not passive in their approach. They are active and willing to jump on their boards, paddle out into the waves, and hang ten regardless of what type of waves come their way.

I've often shared three ways that you will know if your learners are engaged. First of all, they will be asking questions. Engaged learners often seek to know more or go beyond the surface-level information that is being shared. Engaged learners are also active. They are not waiting for someone to tell them what to do next. They seek out opportunities to learn and dive right in. Finally, and you might be able to guess this based on what you've already read throughout this chapter, engaged learners are willing to invest. I've shared this a lot, but it's important to understand that this is what engagement looks like. If they are unwilling to invest, they are not engaged...bottom line.

Considering these levels and understanding where your learners are will help you know what engages them and what is most likely to ignite a willingness to invest. It's not a bad idea to document the level of engagement after a learning experience with your class. This is a way to reflect on what you've designed and consider the impact that it had on your learners.

Engagement vs Entertainment vs Compliance

In closing, it's very important to understand the difference between engagement and entertainment as well as engagement and compliance. While there is nothing wrong with entertainment in the classroom, I believe that learners can be engaged without being entertained. You see, entertainment is about what you do as an educator, engagement is about what they do as a learner. The reality is that a learner can be passive while being entertained but must be active when they are truly engaged (Johnson, 2012).

It's also important to share that compliance does not equal engagement. Just because your learners are looking at you and listening does not mean that they are engaged. They may be well-behaved, but believing that a quiet classroom is an always engaged classroom just doesn't make sense. So, that being said, it is very important that we take the time to consider not only what engagement is but how we can make it a priority in the classroom. Doing so will encourage our learners to actively invest in the learning experiences that we design each and every day.

Reflection Questions

1. On a scale of one to five, how engaged would you say your learners are on a daily basis?

2. What role do you think intentionality plays in engaging today's learners?

3. Out of the Eight Cs of Engagement, which one could you see yourself implementing immediately into your own classroom?

What is your biggest takeaway from Chapter 4?

_____

_____

_____

What challenged or validated something that you already knew?

_____

_____

_____

Works Cited

Johnson, D. (2012, 16 April). *Do we engage or entertain? Education world*. Education World. Retrieved 22 September, 2022, from www.educationworld.com/a_tech/columnists/johnson/johnson026.shtml#:~:text=Entertainment%20results%20through %20the%20creativity.

Peeples, S. (2019, 16 September). *How to create deeper student learning experiences through authentic questions. KQED*. Retrieved 18 May, 2022, from www.kqed.org/mindshift/54378/how-to-create-deeper-student-learning-experiences-through-questions.

Peeples, S. (2019). *Think like Socrates: Using questions to invite wonder and empathy into the classroom, grades 4–12*. Corwin, A Sage Publishing Company.

Schlechty, P.C. (2011). *Engaging students: The next level of working on the work*. Jossey-Bass.

Silver, H., & Perini, M. (2010) *The eight Cs of engagement: How learning styles and instructional design increase student commitment to learning*. Solution Tree. Retrieved from https://smartlib.umri.ac.id/assets/uploads/files/be174-eight-cs-_article.pdf.

What is the QFT?—Right Question Institute. (2018). Right Question Institute. Retrieved from rightquestion.org/what-is-the-qft/.

Section III
Riding the Wave

Chapter 5

Designing the Experience

Designing an experience requires us to consider whether or not what has been designed will leave an impression on our learners.

DOI: 10.4324/9781003349471-8

Just like a surfer that is preparing to ride the waves, our learners will need instruction before being given the opportunity to hop on their boards and test the waters. After igniting a willingness to invest, it's time to provide the opportunity to learn. How will you share the ideas, standards, and concepts that need to be learned by your students? Will they learn by doing? Is explicit instruction necessary to provide information? This part of the framework requires us to provide an experience...in other words, we need to deliver something that will leave an impression on our learners.

Remember, there is a difference between a lesson or activity and an experience. An activity is defined as something that someone or a group does. That's it. So, when you tell your learners that they will be doing an activity, you are basically just letting them know that they will be doing something that day. Who cares, right?

I would be willing to bet that if you asked someone to describe their surfing experience, they would not describe it as an activity. Instead, they would explain it as an experience. There would be inflection in their voice as they shared the excitement and maybe even the fear they encountered as they rode the waves and did something that left an impression on them. They would be amped to help you understand how this experience impacted them and gave them an opportunity to grow as a surfer.

The definition of an experience is something that, as I mentioned previously, leaves an impression. Isn't that what we all want to accomplish as educators? We hope to leave an impression on our learners so that when they walk out of our classrooms each day, the learning goes with them.

Educators often tell me that they weren't trained to design experiences, they were trained to write lesson plans. But I think that when we make statements like this, we are making it harder than it is. I believe that there are four things that we should consider when designing an experience...

1. Will this experience leave an impression on my learners? In other words, will they walk out of the classroom and still be thinking about/talking about what they've learned?
2. Does this learning experience give my learners an opportunity to practice life-ready and social-emotional learning skills? As I mentioned in Chapter 4, this can make learning more authentic and has the potential to ignite a willingness to invest.
3. Will this experience challenge every learner in some way? This can be difficult but it's the reason that designing for depth is so important. When our learners are challenged, they grow. When they grow, they begin to reach the deep understanding that we know is so important.
4. After this experience, will my learners be able to apply what they've learned? Application is important and this will make more sense when we explore Webb's Depth of Knowledge in Chapter 7.

If we want to take this idea a little bit further, we might consider: will the experience leave an impression on my gifted learners and high achievers? Will the experience leave an impression on my struggling learners? Will the experience leave an impression on my learners who fall somewhere in between? These are the questions that will result in intentional and purposeful learning experiences. Ultimately, we should want our learners to go home and talk about what they've experienced that day at school.

Our words matter. Instead of sitting down to write a lesson plan or even create an activity, remind yourself that you are preparing to design meaningful learning experiences for your students. Simply utilizing the right words when describing or explaining our actions can make a difference. I have had many educators tell me that this mindset shift, in and of itself, has had a huge impact on their practice.

If you're like me, it might be difficult to think about practical ways to make this a reality. While I wanted everything that I did to leave an impression on my learners, I sometimes found it difficult to know what that looked like. I wanted my learners to go home and talk about what we did in class every single day. I know that so often when our learners are asked at home what happened at school, they respond with, "Nothing." We all know that this isn't the case but what they really mean is that "I didn't do anything that I want to talk about, I didn't do anything that was meaningful to me, and I didn't do anything that makes me want to go back tomorrow." Ouch, right?

The problem with the experiences that many of our gifted learners encounter in the classroom is the level of depth. As we discussed in Chapter 2, it's easy to just provide enough information for our learners to experience surface-level learning rather than a deep understanding of the content. But, the problem with that approach is that there are some of our learners that already have that surface-level perspective before they even step into our classrooms.

The Power of PBL

So, in this chapter, we will explore several ways that we can provide an experience that will leave a lasting impression on all of our learners. And, you probably saw this coming, but I think our first consideration should be the implementation of some type of project-based learning experience. I've talked about this in every book that I've written, but that's simply because project-based learning, or PBL, gives learners the opportunity to experience content in a way that makes sense for them as individual learners.

One of the things that I love most about PBL is the variety of ways that we, as educators, can make it happen in our classrooms. Project-based learning, the OG, is often the opportunity for learners to work on a project that has been created or designed by their teacher. Problem-based learning gives learners the opportunity to solve a real problem, and passion-based learning gives them the opportunity to make an impact or create real change by pursuing their own passions and interests.

PBLworks.org is one of my favorite resources for everything PBL. I love that they explain the difference between dessert and main course projects (PBLWorks, 2019). They explain that there is a difference between "doing a project" and "project-based learning." I could not agree more with this perspective as I've seen learners that are simply doing a project and I've also seen learners that are experiencing project-based learning. Those that are simply doing a project are typically not as invested because they don't see it as an opportunity to understand the content. Instead, they are utilizing what they've already learned to create something that they may or may not find value in. In short, there is a difference and that difference is important for us to understand as educators.

You see, project-based learning gives learners the opportunity to experience the learning and understand the content through working on the project. Instead of seeing the project as a way to "wrap up" the unit of study or busy-work for those that already understand, educators with this perspective understand that, when designed well, a project can give learners the opportunity to not only learn the content but reach a deep understanding of the concepts, standards, and skills that are woven into the learning experience.

PBL Baby Steps

I was recently asked how to implement the elements of a project-based learning experience in a manageable way. This question was asked by an administrator who wanted her staff to consider this type of learning but didn't want to overwhelm them by asking them to make it happen overnight. In response to that question, I created the Project-Based Learning Baby Steps (McNair, 2020).

Outside Experts	Reflection	Product Creation
Invite an outside expert to connect with your class and share their experience	Encourage your learners to reflect on a learning experience and share that reflection with others.	Challenge learners to create a product to demonstrate what they've learned.
Curiosity	**Connections**	**Authentic Audience**
Ignite curiosity by asking learners what they want to know about a concept standard, or idea.	Ask learners to make cross-curricular connections as well as connections to life beyond the walls of the classroom.	Encourage learners to share their learning or explain their learning to someone else.
Essential Questions	**Life-Ready Skills**	**Empathy**
Develop essential questions as a class before exploring a particular concept, idea, or standard.	Utilize life-ready skills while working on a project to make the experience more authentic.	Ask learners to use what they've learned to create change or make an impact beyond the classroom.

PBL Baby Steps
STARTING SMALL TO CULTIVATE A PBL
MINDSET INTO YOUR CLASSROOM CULTURE

Figure 5.1. PBL Baby Steps.

Just as there are different ways to ride a wave, there are different ways for us, as educators, to design experiences that our learners will remember beyond the walls of the classroom. Some of us take an all-in approach and will jump on the board without any fear or hesitancy. Others want to practice on the shore and really have a feel for what it will look like and feel like before going all in.

Each one of the baby steps is, in and of itself, a way to turn an activity into an experience. These are a great way for those that aren't ready to go all in to get started. Let's talk through these and the impact that they can have in the classroom when they are used in a way that makes sense.

1. Outside experts—Outside experts are a great way to give your learners a different perspective on what is being learned. Sometimes, just hearing a different voice and hearing from someone that uses that skill, standard, or concept every day beyond the walls of the classroom can have a huge impact on our learners.
2. Reflection—We are going to dive into reflection later in the book when we consider how to empower our learners to utilize what they have learned. But, at its core, reflection encourages learners to consider what they've learned and what it means to them.
3. Product creation—Creating a product is a hallmark of the project-based learning strategy and gives learners the opportunity to apply what they've learned through design and application.
4. Curiosity—We talked a lot about curiosity in Chapter 3 as we discussed how to engage today's learners at the beginning of a learning experience. Curiosity is the fuel that keeps our learners invested in the experience. Without curiosity, learners are often learning out of compliance and will not be truly engaged.

5. Connections—A learning experience that prioritizes connections beyond the walls of the classroom will result in the learning feeling authentic…real. The collision of classroom content and beyond the classroom experiences is the sweet spot of education and should be valued and implemented as often as possible.

6. Authentic audience—I happen to believe that it's important for our learners to share their work out with the world. Today's learners are familiar with creating for an audience because of their experience with social media. If we can teach them to use those platforms to promote themselves positively, we will be preparing them to do big things beyond the walls of the classroom.

7. Essential questions—Essential questions help our learners understand the big idea of a learning experience. Creating an essential question requires them to think beyond factual questions and mundane information. Instead, they are encouraged to consider overarching questions that might even lead to more questions.

8. Life-ready skills—As I shared earlier, any time you weave life-ready skills into a learning experience, it makes the learning more authentic and relevant. These skills can include anything that a learner will likely use beyond the walls of the classroom.

9. Empathy—As a fan of passion-based learning, this is one of my favorite baby steps. Giving our learners the opportunity to look beyond themselves and into the world around them to recognize something that they'd like to change to make the world a better place for someone else is a win-win and something that they will always remember.

The PBL Baby Steps are basically innovative solutions and ideas that can be implemented into any learning experience at any time. I've created this as a choice board so that it can be used in a variety of ways. I once had someone share with me that they were going to challenge their educators to get a tic-tac-toe by taking the risk to implement at least three of the baby steps throughout one semester.

Instructional specialists might also use this collection of ideas to consider how they might encourage educators to explore innovative ideas to help their learners make connections and invest in what is being learned.

Asking the Wrong Question

John Hattie shares that his work, Visible Learning, "is a deliberate mindset that shifts the focus from what teachers are teaching to what students are learning (Corwin, 2020, p. 2)." So often, we ask ourselves, "How will we *teach* this idea, concept, or standard?" In doing so, we are putting a lot of pressure on ourselves and assuming that simply because it's taught, it will be learned. It's a better idea and I would even say best practice to instead ask, "How will they *learn and ultimately understand* this idea, concept, or standard?" Do you see the difference?

If we consider what we hope the outcome will be, it is that our students understand what is being shared. The reality is that it doesn't matter how we teach it if it doesn't result in them learning it and it doesn't matter if they've learned it if they don't understand it. Asking this question before sitting down to design any experience can put us in the right frame of mind to focus on a way that will result in experiences that will provide a return on our investment.

The Importance of Variety

In considering the experiences that we provide in the classroom, it's important to make variety a priority. While there is something to be said for consistency and routine, it's also important to recognize that when the classroom experience becomes mundane, our learners will disengage. When things become boring, our learners will begin to lack interest and excitement. It makes sense that if that becomes the reality, our learners won't want to invest, and to be honest, neither will we.

The attention span of today's learners isn't getting any longer and while I think giving them opportunities to work on that is not a bad idea, I also think that we would be silly to ignore the fact that they spend most of their time swiping through videos that are 3 minutes at the absolute most…I'm looking at you, TikTok.

More than any generation before, these guys have access to a never-ending variety of content, entertainment, and random information. I, myself, find it difficult to watch an entire movie after spending time on my mobile device. I just don't feel like I have time for it and I am frustrated when they don't get to the point in a reasonable amount of time.

The Opportunity to Struggle

When designing an experience, it's important to consider the opportunity for your learners to experience productive struggle. Yes, I used the word opportunity and struggle in the same sentence. I learned quickly with my gifted learners that many of them had no idea how to struggle. In fact, when they did experience struggle they almost instantly had a meltdown and completely disengaged from the work. This, in and of itself, made it very clear that school was something that they expected to be easy. In fact, many of them didn't even like the idea of putting forth effort when they were challenged in any way, shape, or form.

Productive struggle is a valuable part of the learning process. I would even go out on a limb and say that it's one of the most valuable parts of the learning process. Think about yourself and how much you learn when something comes easy or you are able to do it with little or no effort. Then consider how much you learn when you are forced to work hard or do more because of the challenge that the situation brings. I would be willing to bet that, like me, you learn more when you have to put forth more effort because the reality is that you are required to invest more by doing so.

One of the articles that I read about surfing while writing this book stated that "if you aren't getting wiped out, it is quite possible that you aren't pushing yourself hard enough" (Gupta, 2016), and I absolutely love that. If our learners are riding the waves every day in the classroom without wiping out, it's too easy...we aren't challenging them enough. We will talk more about this idea in Chapter 9, but the reality is that every surfer wipes out at some point. It's how they react and respond to that wipeout that matters.

Reflection Questions

1. How big of an impact do you think shifting from writing lesson plans to designing experiences might have in your classroom?

2. How often do you feel like what you do in your classroom leaves an impression on your learners?

3. Which of the PBL Baby Steps do you think you could implement immediately into your classroom to make learning an experience?

What is your biggest takeaway from Chapter 5?

_____

_____

_____

What challenged or validated something that you already knew?

_____

_____

_____

Works Cited

Corwin (2020). Powerful professional learning. Retrieved 23 November, 2022, from https://us.corwin.com/sites/default/ files/vl_program_guide_2020_vln19675.pdf.

PBLWorks (2019). *"Doing a project" vs. project-based learning.* Retrieved from www.pblworks.org/doing-project-vs-project-based-learning.

Gupta, S. (2016, 19 October). *Types of surfing wipeouts.* Red Bull. Retrieved 18 May, 2022, from www.redbull.com/in-en/ types-of-surfing-wipeouts.

McNair, A. (2022, 14 December). *PBL baby steps.* A Meaningful Mess. Retrieved 17 May, 2022, from www.andimcnair.com/ andis-blog/december-14th-2020.

Chapter 6

Beyond the Classroom Walls

BIG IDEA

Empowering learners to utilize what has been learned is about helping them make connections to what they experience in the classroom and what they experience beyond the classroom.

DOI: 10.4324/9781003349471-9

After providing the opportunity to learn, it's important to empower your learners to apply what they've learned beyond the walls of the classroom. As a generation, today's learners have unlimited access to information. If they are coming to school, only to be given the information that they can Google or find anywhere on the internet, they are going to be frustrated and disengaged.

However, if we can help them, not only learn the content but also make connections to how they can use what they've learned beyond the walls of the classroom, the learning becomes purposeful and meaningful. That's what this part of the framework is all about. How can I help my learners consider how they will utilize what they've learned beyond the walls of the classroom?

Just like igniting a willingness to invest, this important part of a learning experience can often be overlooked. Instead, we often deliver the content, check for understanding, and move on. While that method may result in surface-level learning and the ability to regurgitate information, it will rarely result in the deep understanding that is necessary for our learners to be able to apply what has been learned.

Not empowering our learners to apply what they've learned is the equivalent of someone learning to surf on the sand and never getting out into the water. There's no opportunity to apply or do something with what has been learned. The learning may make sense but until they are given the opportunity to utilize it on their own terms, it simply seems like random information.

There are so many ways that we can make this part of the learning experience a priority without feeling as if we are adding something extra to the plate. Empowering our learners to take ownership can be done through intentional and purposeful reflection woven throughout or encouraged at the end of a learning experience, encouraging school-to-home connections, giving your learners the opportunity to share what they've learned with others, and providing choice. As I shared earlier, in many of the classrooms that I visit, there is sometimes a hook and usually an opportunity to learn the content. However, there is not always an opportunity to internalize what was learned so that it will stick with them.

Empowerment through Reflection

Let's start with the importance of making reflection a priority in the classroom. Reflecting on what has been learned is essential for today's learners. Simply remembering things isn't necessary because they have the ability to Google anything from anywhere. However, reflection requires them to see things from a deeper perspective. It encourages them to personalize the learning and really think through how they will utilize what they've learned beyond the walls of the classroom.

Reflecting doesn't require a great deal of time or extra work to implement, but make no mistake, if reflection is not prioritized, your learners will walk out of your classroom and it will be as if it never happened. It's easy to see reflection as an "extra" piece or something that may happen if there is extra time at the end of class. But, here's the thing...reflection is not extra, it's essential. When we reflect, we find value in what has been learned and realize why it matters to us as individuals.

One of my favorite ways to encourage student reflection is through a tool that my friend, Kari Espin, and I call the Reflection Triangle. The Reflection Triangle encourages learners to consider what they've learned and what it means to them. Let me show you what this looks like...

In the bottom three boxes, you might ask your learners to share three things that they learned from a particular experience.

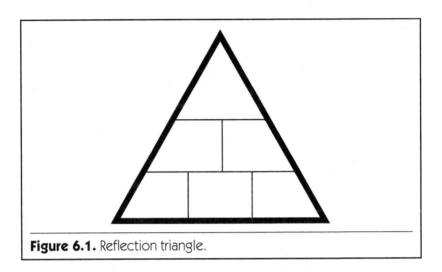

Figure 6.1. Reflection triangle.

Next, they would identify two things that they can do because of what they've learned, and finally, they would document one question that they still have.

To take this type of reflection one step further, you could have your learners put their triangles together to collaborate and see the learning from a different perspective. When the two triangles are put together, learners might compare what they've learned and what questions they still have. It's a possibility that one learner's question might be something that the other student learned. I love this experience simply because it helps learners recognize that everyone rides the waves differently and if we take the time to do so, we can learn from everyone's experience.

Consider what reflection looks like beyond the walls of the classroom. So often, when we experience something that we enjoy or we feel like others might benefit from, and we can't wait to share it. We talk about it from our own perspectives and share the impact that it had. This is exactly what should happen as we encourage our learners to reflect.

Reserving the last three to five minutes of class for reflection will ensure that your learners do not leave without an

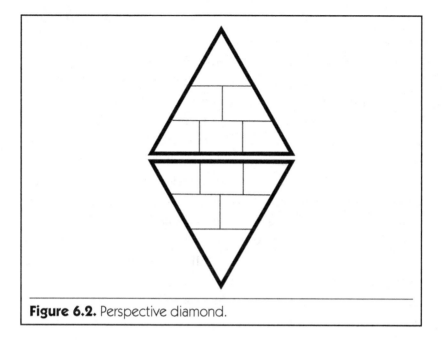

Figure 6.2. Perspective diamond.

understanding of how what they've learned that day connects to life beyond the walls of the classroom. This gives them an opportunity to internalize what has been learned and when this happens, there is a much better chance that they will keep it in their basket and remember it long after it has been experienced in the classroom.

Empowerment through Connections

Empowering learners to make the connection between who they are at home and who they are at school is essential. One of the first clues that we aren't doing this well is when we, as educators, or our learners refer to anything that happens outside of school as the "real world." If school isn't the real world, then what is it? Shouldn't school, at the very least, align with what our learners experience beyond the walls of the classroom? Using the phrase "real world" implies and supports the idea that school is somehow completely disconnected and I would think might send a very confusing message. I mean, if I'm a learner and my teacher talks about the "real world", I would be wondering where in the world I was right now if not in the "real world." Have we become so driven by standardized test scores that we aren't concerned about the fact that our learners don't have the skills that they will need for the majority of their lives that will be spent outside of the classroom?

I was at lunch recently with Jessica Torres, a good friend and colleague of mine. We were talking about the importance of connections and she shared that she thinks it's so important that we are willing to help learners to make connections to *their* lives beyond the walls of the classroom rather than what we think their lives beyond the walls of the classroom should be. In other words, our life experience is not always their life experience. And in order to make connections that are meaningful to them, we have to be willing to look beyond what we think things should be and into what they actually are.

Let me give you an example of this. My boys absolutely love baseball. As a family, we practically live at the baseball fields during the spring season. Anyone that watches baseball or has any interest in the sport at all recognizes the number of connections that can be made to mathematics. Baseball is a game that involves statistics. Any opportunity that I can find to help my boys understand a mathematics concept through a baseball concept is going to be meaningful. For example, knowing their batting average is always important for a baseball player. If I knew this information as an educator and we were learning about ratio, average, or even decimals in the classroom that week, I might challenge them to figure out their batting average and bring it to class the next day.

Without school-to-home connections, learners will walk out of your classroom and never think about what you've taught them again. They will get on their phones or their parent's phones and access what they consider to be meaningful content. And, let's be honest, they are going to do that anyway. So, if we can help them connect what they've learned in the classroom to what they access outside of the classroom, it's a win-win. Again, it doesn't matter whether or not we think this content is meaningful…it matters what they think is meaningful.

Empowerment through the Protégé Effect

Being given the opportunity to share what is being learned with others can result in a deep understanding. We know that the protégé effect can have a big impact on our learners and when used well, it can result in a meaningful experience for everyone involved. The protégé effect represents the idea that the best way to learn is to teach. This idea was developed by Jean-Pol Martin in the 1980s (*Learn better, by teaching*, 2020).

I know that this is true from personal experience. So often, I understand something from a completely different perspective after being given the opportunity to share it with educators. There's just something about teaching others that gives learning the opportunity to sink in and helps me understand.

The key to making the protégé effect work is being sure that both learners involved understand the value of their role in the experience. When gifted learners feel as if they are just being used to teach another student, they will almost always become frustrated and realize that there are better ways for them to spend their time. However, if they understand that the experience will deepen their understanding, they might be more willing to actively invest.

Empowerment through Choice

Giving our learners choices regarding how they will demonstrate what they've learned and how they will use what they've learned to demonstrate understanding is another way to give our learners ownership and put them in the driver's seat.

I don't believe that we have to always provide choice as I know that there are times in the classroom when it's important that learners can demonstrate understanding in a specific way. However, I do think that the more often we can give them the opportunity to practice autonomy through making a choice, the better.

I was recently having a conversation with educators that were feeling overwhelmed with creating choice boards. They said the thought of coming up with nine different choices felt like a lot of work that would require a lot of extra time. I explained to them that choice doesn't always have to look like a tic-tac-toe board. Giving learners the opportunity to choose between two or three ideas is still a choice. Ian Byrd helped me understand this through his post, Choice Menus: Quality or Mere Quantity (Byrd, 2019).

The important thing to consider when giving our learners choices is to be sure that the choices that are given represent different perspectives and different ways of doing things. If the choices are too similar, it won't actually feel like they are being given a choice at all.

Empowering your learners is ultimately about being intentional about helping them utilize what they've learned. It makes no sense to learn something and not be able to do something with it. Whether you do this through reflection, personal connections, the protégé effect, or student choice, this part of a learning experience should help our learners understand the why.

Reflection Questions

1. How much of a priority is reflection in your classroom?

2. How can you help your learners make connections between what is being learned at school and their lives beyond the walls of the classroom?

3. How might you effectively utilize the protégé effect in your own classroom?

What is your biggest takeaway from Chapter 6?

_____

_____

_____

What challenged or validated something that you already knew?

_____

_____

_____

Works Cited

Byrd, I. (2019, 7 June). *Choice menus: Quality or mere quantity.* Byrdseed.com. Retrieved from https://www.byrdseed.com/extension-menus-redux/#why.

Learn better, by teaching. (2020, 26 May). Kaplan.co.uk. Retrieved from kaplan.co.uk/insights/article-detail/insights/2020/05/25/learn-better-by-teaching.

Chapter 7

Knowing What They Need

BIG IDEA

Taking the time to consider what our learners understand will give us the evidence that we need to determine what they need moving forward.

DOI: 10.4324/9781003349471-10

The three pieces that I shared in the previous chapters, engage, experience, and empower, are key to any learning experience and should be designed in a way that will leave an impression. However, if we stop here, we are missing the opportunity to design for depth; instead, we are simply designing an experience and hoping that it will meet the needs of all of our learners.

Differentiation often seems stressful because we sometimes assume that we need to plan different experiences for different types of learners. I don't think this is the case. In fact, my suggestion is to plan one meaningful experience and then intentionally consider what you will do for your learners that are struggling to understand and those that are ready to dive deeper into the learning.

Looking for Evidence

As I watched video after video of surfers riding the waves to prepare for this project, it became obvious that every surfer approached the waves differently. As I watched, I could tell that some of them were novices. They looked shaky, inexperienced, and unsure about what was coming their way. Others were experts. They looked steady, confident, and completely comfortable with every challenge that the ocean brought their way.

The point here is that I had to observe closely and pay attention. I think that when we do those two things, it's easier than we sometimes assume to know what learners need. As I watched the videos of those that were learning to surf, they often sometimes started out with an instructor in a pool that simulated the ocean. That instructor watched them closely and provided feedback as they practiced what they were being told to do. This real-time feedback helped the surfer make immediate corrections in the moment rather than waiting until the end of the experience to fix something that they may or may not even realize that they were doing wrong. Sounds a bit like formative assessment, yes? They also used explicit instruction and actively demonstrated what they are expecting their student surfer to do.

What Is Evidence?

After providing the core learning experience (*engage, experience,* and *empower*), it's important to consider the *evidence.* How will you know that your learners understand what has been learned? What will they be able to do? How will you check for deep understanding and how will you know if they've moved beyond surface-level learning?

This is often referred to as success criteria and shared with learners before they engage in the learning experience. The Teaching Channel explains that "Success criteria really provides students with an opportunity to assess their own learning" (Freibrun, 2021). It is exactly what it sounds like as it provides the criteria for both the teacher and the learner to use to determine success.

I would imagine that one of the hardest things for a surfing instructor to do is to turn a novice surfer loose in the ocean to experience the waves on their own. I'm sure that they fully recognize that there will be many wipeouts before surfing success is achieved. However, they also know that the wipeouts will make the moment that they are able to ride a stellar wave even sweeter. They focus on the outcome rather than focusing on the number of wipeouts that it takes to achieve success.

Make no mistake, the instructor and the surfer understand what success will eventually look like. If they didn't, there would be nothing to work toward. But, the novice surfer has probably spent time watching videos of many successful rides. They know that, when they get it right, riding the waves will look and feel a specific way.

As I watched the surfers, I became more familiar with what a well-executed ride looked like. It was important to consider the complexity and size of the wave, the experience of the surfer, and ultimately their approach to the challenge. But, as I watched them, I realized that doing so was much like considering the evidence before determining what our learners need next in the classroom.

The Value of Self-Assessment

One of my favorite ways to gather evidence is through self-assessment. Self-assessment requires learners to move from the passenger seat into the driver's seat and vice versa for the educator. Giving your learners an opportunity to tell you whether or not they understand what has been learned is a great way to encourage self-awareness, an important social-emotional learning skill that can be applied far beyond the walls of the classroom.

A self-assessment can be filled out as an exit ticket on paper or digitally, using Google Forms. Utilizing Google Forms will make the disaggregation of the responses more manageable for you. There are four questions that I think should be asked for learners to self-assess:

1. What went well as you worked on this experience?—
This question is important because it gives every learner
an opportunity to celebrate their success. Even if they

struggled through the experience, the hope is that they can identify one thing that they feel they did well.

2. What was difficult as you worked on this experience? —This question might be difficult for gifted learners to answer. They often don't like to admit when something is hard because they are afraid that it will result in someone perceiving them differently than they did before. However, being able to share our struggles is an important part of the learning process and should be encouraged. And, if the answer to this question is consistently nothing, you will know that, as the educator, you are not challenging your learners appropriately.

3. On a scale of one to four, how would you rate your understanding of the experience? —This is my favorite question simply because I believe it is the question that makes differentiation more manageable. This takes the guesswork out of the equation and gives learners the opportunity to tell you what they need in order to move forward in a way that will result in deep understanding.

4. What questions do you still have? —This question encourages a growth mindset and helps our learners understand that it's okay to still have questions after a learning experience. This can also lead to an opportunity for learners to dive deeper through exploring their questions when there is a time and space to do so.

Looking at the results of the form filled out by your learners on a Google Sheet, you will be able to see who is ready for surface-level learning and who is ready to dive into deep understanding. If they rate themselves a one or a two, they will need extra support. If they rate themselves a three or a four, they will need an extension.

I like this idea because as I shared earlier, I think many educators feel like differentiation is a guessing game and this simplifies the process and helps our learners focus on their own experiences and what they need.

Utilizing Depth of Knowledge

I think that oftentimes, we teach with a checklist mindset. We have a list of standards that we are required to teach and we do so, assuming that if they can pass the unit test or regurgitate what was shared on a worksheet that they understand. However, I want to push back on that idea in the hopes that we can agree on the difference between learning and understanding.

There is a place for both in the classroom. Both learning something and understanding it is important. But the definition of learning is "the acquisition of knowledge or skills through experience, study, or by being taught." Remember, just because we teach something doesn't even mean that they've learned it, much less understood it. One definition of understanding is to "perceive the significance, explanation, or cause of (something)." This is my favorite of the definitions because I have a hard time believing that our learners will be willing to invest if they do not see the significance in what is being learned.

Knowing what to provide as extra support and as an extension becomes the next important conversation. In order to make this part of a learning experience meaningful, we must be intentional, or it will feel as if we are spinning our wheels.

Whether you utilize the self-assessment that I shared previously in this chapter, or another form of formative assessment to determine what your learners need, it's important to carefully consider their feedback. There are lots of ways to provide extra support to learners that do not understand. But, the reality is that there are varying levels of understanding. It's important to know what deep understanding looks like for the specific standard, concept, or idea being learned. As I shared earlier, when we discussed evidence, I think this is best accomplished through self-assessment or the opportunity to actually do something with what they've learned through application.

Webb's Depth of Knowledge Framework (Hammer, 2018) makes a lot of sense and helps our learners recognize where they are versus where they want to go. I do not believe that every learner should be expected to be at Level Four all of the time. Instead, I think a fluid approach is a much better idea. It's important to identify where learners are as far as understanding goes and then consider the best plan for getting them to the place that you'd like for them to be.

The reality is that many of our classrooms only give learners the opportunity to experience Level One of the Depth of Knowledge Framework—Recall and Reproduction. They are spoon-fed the information and then expected to remember that content and regurgitate it on the unit test to demonstrate understanding. However, let's be honest. That's not understanding. That's surface-level learning that will only be remembered for a very limited amount of time.

The second level of Depth of Knowledge is Basic Application of Skills and Concepts. I want to be clear. When I talk about deep understanding of what has been learned through application, I am not talking about this level. While I believe that this level is where many learners should start, it cannot be seen as the endgame if we are looking for a real, deep understanding of what has been learned.

Strategic Thinking is the third level and really begins to provide learners with the opportunity to think beyond the surface. This requires them to think about how they might be able to utilize what has been learned and how it might apply to their own lives beyond the walls of the classroom. I believe that this is key and it's why the *empower* piece is such an important part of learning design. Being intentional about this reminds us to give every learner an opportunity to dive into the learning from a perspective that is meaningful and will make the learning stick.

The last level, Level Four, involves Extended Thinking. This is what we want our learners to achieve in order to demonstrate a deep understanding of a standard, concept, or idea. This means that they can not only apply what they learned but utilize it to create and design something new. I think that we often assume our learners are not capable of understanding at this level. We are afraid to give them the autonomy and independence that this level requires. However, at some point, they've got to stand up on their boards and tackle the big waves. This is an opportunity to allow them to do that. Trust me, when that moment happens and you see them out there, fully invested, all in and riding the waves, you will realize that this is the sweet spot... this is what it's about.

Determining whether a learner needs extra support or an extension often begins with deciding what they are able to do within the Depth of Knowledge Framework. This framework makes a lot of sense and provides perspective regarding what to ask learners to do, regardless of what level they are able to achieve.

Types of Motivation

Along with knowing what our learners will need as far as differentiation goes, it's also important to understand what motivates them. I think we often forget the importance of intrinsic motivation in the classroom. When used appropriately, intrinsic motivation has the potential to turn a surfer that only hits the waves because of the attention that they receive into a soul surfer that surfs because the ocean is where they feel most at home and in their element.

In his book, *Drive: The Surprising Truth about Motivation*, Daniel Pink shares that there are three elements of true motivation, mastery, autonomy, and purpose (Pink, 2009). After learning about this, I have started paying attention to the educators that I work with as well as the students that they serve. In doing so, I've realized that this is extremely accurate. If I take the time to figure out what motivates the educator that I'm working with, we both have a much better experience.

I've also noticed that the educators that I see prioritize these things in their classroom simply have better engagement and their learners seem more authentically invested than those that don't. Their learners seem to want to be in the classroom more than those that prioritize extrinsic motivation.

Motivating through Autonomy

Autonomy involves giving your learners choices and the opportunity to practice independence. Often, we feel as if we need to tell our learners how to think, what to do, and when to do it. What if instead, we gave them the opportunity to make some of those decisions? What if we trusted them enough to provide choice? I recognize that there are some parts of the school day that are not conducive to an autonomous approach. But we can't be frustrated with them as a generation for not being able to make decisions when they are rarely given the opportunity to do so.

Motivating through Mastery

Mastering a concept, strategy, or skill can be very rewarding. In fact, some of our learners are driven by the idea of mastery. They love nothing more than to learn all that they can and then use what they've learned to accomplish a goal. I can think of many of my gifted learners that loved demonstrating and showing me when they had reached mastery. They would be so proud and for as long as I would listen, they would tell me everything that they already knew and had learned along the way.

Motivating through Purpose

Finally, purpose gives learners a reason to engage in what is being shared. This happens to be my favorite and in my opinion, the most important of the three drivers for intrinsic motivation. Without purpose, it's hard to understand why anything should be a priority. Personally, purpose is what motivates me and without it, I find it very difficult to invest.

Considering these levels and understanding where your learners are will help you know what engages them and what is most likely to ignite a willingness to invest. Earlier in the book I shared that it's not a bad idea to document the level of engagement after a learning experience with your class. You could take this idea a bit further by considering what type of intrinsic motivation you saw from your learners and utilizing this information to make connections in the future. This is a way to reflect on what you've designed and consider the impact that it had on your learners.

Often, we overlook the importance of this part of designing a learning experience. We know how important it is that we deliver the content, but we simply forget that without considering the motivation that is driving their willingness to invest, our learners will not engage in the opportunity to learn that will provide the content and information that is needed to move forward. Looking for evidence is how we make decisions about what learners will need and how we can ensure that they will reach the level of understanding that is most appropriate. Knowing what motivates them provides clarity and will help us truly understand who they are as learners so that we can move them from the beach out into the waves that truly prepare them to become the lifelong learners that we know that they can be.

Reflection Questions

1. What evidence do you use in your classroom to know what your learners will need beyond the initial learning experience?

2. How much of a priority is extrinsic motivation in your classroom? How much of a priority is intrinsic motivation?

3. What motivates you as a learner?

What is your biggest takeaway from Chapter 7?

_____

_____

_____

What challenged or validated something that you already knew?

_____

_____

_____

Works Cited

Freibrun, M. (2021, 12 October). *Using success criteria to spark motivation in your students.* www.teachingchannel.com. Retrieved from www.teachingchannel.com/blog/success-criteria.

Hammer, B. (2018, August). *Webb's depth of knowledge framework: The basics.* Edmentum.com. blog.edmentum.com/webb%E2%80%99s-depth-knowledge-framework-basics.

Pink, D. H. (2009). *Drive: The surprising truth about what motivates us.* Canongate Books Ltd.

Section IV

Creating Soul Surfers

Chapter 8

Providing Depth through Extension

BIG IDEA

The Depth and Complexity Icons provide educators with practical ideas to use as a way of extending the learning and adding depth to any standard, concept, or idea.

DOI: 10.4324/9781003349471-12

After it's been established whether a learner needs extra support or an extension experience through the evidence, it's important that we focus on what we are trying to achieve. Remember, the goal should be for every learner to learn and understand. Let me explain.

I often remember the difference between learning and understanding by remembering that learning is more about the what and understanding is more about the how and the why. The what is important and definitely a starting place, but if we never get to the how and the why, we will be missing an opportunity for our learners to make the connections that are necessary to experience a deep understanding of the content, idea, or standard.

If a learner has reached a place in the learning journey where they have not only learned the content but understood it, it's important to consider how that understanding can be extended. This can happen through exploration, independent study, or purposeful opportunities to learn from a deeper, more complex perspective. In this chapter, we will explore practical and manageable ways to provide depth and complexity.

The Depth and Complexity Icons

The Depth and Complexity Icons are a purposeful way to make learning meaningful for students that are ready to move beyond the surface level. In fact, it's not a bad idea to weave these icons into every experience for every learner. However, I want to introduce them as options to consider when you are intentionally designing for depth. In this chapter, I will explain each of the icons as well as provide a variety of ways that they can be introduced and implemented in any classroom.

As we all know, icons and images are a great way to help our learners make connections. In this case, the icons prompt learners to think in a specific way. Created in 1994 by Sandra Kaplan and Bette Gould, the Depth and Complexity Icons give learners the tools and strategies to think like an expert. On her website, Envision Gifted, Marcie Griffith explains that

> The Depth and Complexity Icons are visual prompts designed to help students go beyond surface level understanding of a concept and enhance their ability to think critically. These critical thinking tools help students dig deeper into a concept (*depth*) and understand that concept with greater *complexity*.
>
> (*Griffith, n.d.*)

I utilized the Depth and Complexity Icons in my classroom with my gifted learners. One of the things that I realized fairly early on is that I could have been using these icons with any of my learners (gifted or not) to encourage them to think differently and deeply about a concept, idea, or standard that I needed them to understand.

As I began to utilize the icons, I realized that my learners began to respond and utilize their critical thinking skills to make connections to whatever was being learned and the icon that was being implemented. After using them for a couple of weeks, I was convinced that the icons were super valuable and should be prioritized. So, in this chapter, I want to take the time to introduce each of the icons and talk about how they can be used to extend learning for those that are ready to dive deeper.

When I decided to include a chapter in this book regarding the Depth and Complexity Icons, I knew that I wanted Marcy Voss to share her thoughts. Marcy recently retired after 36 years in public education. During her career, she coordinated gifted and special programs in several districts, as well as served on the Commissioner's Gifted and Talented Advisory Council and the TAGT Board. Marcy is the author of the best-selling *Q3 Depth and Complexity Question Stem Cards*. The TALK Cards (Gould, 2019), her latest Depth and Complexity publication, focuses on the alignment of Depth and Complexity with ELLs and language acquisition. I've learned so much from her regarding Depth and Complexity and it only made sense for me to ask her to share her expertise in this chapter.

Marcy's Perspective

As a new G/T teacher in the 1980s, I was told I should increase the rigor of my curriculum and instruction by making it more in-depth and complex. But no one told me how to do this. So, I was excited to learn about the elements/icons of Depth and Complexity from Sandra Kaplan in the late 1990s. This set of thinking tools, developed by Kaplan, Bette Gould, and Sheila Madsen, provides a concrete way for teachers to manipulate curriculum and instruction so students can think about content in more in-depth, complex ways, as well as a way for students to structure their own learning process.

I learned that I could begin introducing the elements/icons by making connections to places where they fit in my existing curriculum. For example, students already had experience with math and spelling patterns. They could use text evidence (details) to draw conclusions or determine the theme of the story (big ideas). Once students became familiar with the elements, I could stretch their thinking by combining multiple elements, such as having students use the language of a mathematician to explain the patterns found in rules for solving linear and nonlinear equations or look at changes over time in the patterns of the western settlement to create a generalization regarding westward expansion.

I learned I could tier my activities and questions by providing different levels of in-depth, complex thinking related to a topic for students with different abilities. For example, a level 1 activity might ask students to analyze features or recurring events in elections. In a level 2 activity, students might analyze the ongoing factors that influenced elections over time. Students completing a level 3 activity might analyze dilemmas or controversies in elections from multiple perspectives.

I also learned I could address the needs of my gifted emergent bilingual students by combining sheltered instruction with Depth and Complexity. One way I could do this is by providing a sentence stem that requires the use of academic vocabulary and in-depth, complex thinking. For example, the stem "One generalization that summarizes how living organisms within an ecosystem interact with one another and their environment is ___," requires that students use academic vocabulary such as "organisms" and "ecosystem" while they identify the big idea of the lesson. I could have students use this stem in a Turn and Talk or Parallel Line activity so they could practice speaking using the academic vocabulary as they listen to others' ideas. Or I could provide another sheltered strategy, such as the use of visuals, and ask students to think about them using the elements of Depth and Complexity. For example, I could show a picture of the Civil War and ask students to collaborate to analyze details that might provide different perspectives on the war.

But, more importantly, I learned that as students gained experience with the model of Depth and Complexity, I could turn over the learning to them. I could allow the students to determine the type of thinking they would do as they investigated the curriculum, or I could ask them to find a way to relate their learning to Depth and Complexity.

Over the years, I have seen how teachers trained in the use of this model have transformed education for gifted students. Gifted classrooms are no longer comprised of fun activities and games without purpose. Students are empowered to take ownership of their learning, creating excitement and engagement. Teachers are amazed at the type of thinking their students can do, including their twice exceptional and gifted emergent bilingual students. In the 40+ years I have been involved in gifted education, I have not seen another model so effectively address the advanced learning needs of gifted students, nor have I seen a model that is so versatile, offering endless ways for teachers to present rigorous and challenging instruction adapted to the individual needs of their learners.

Now that you have been introduced to the concept of the Depth and Complexity Icons and have had the opportunity to read about the big picture of how they might be implemented in the classroom, let me introduce the icons. There are 11 icons in all. Eight of the icons encourage learners to think more deeply and three of the icons encourage them to focus on complexity. The Depth Icons include:

- Language of the Discipline
- Details
- Trends
- Patterns
- Rules
- Ethics
- Unanswered Questions
- Big Ideas

The Complexity Icons include:

- Changes Over Time
- Multiple Perspectives
- Across Disciplines

You can find the icons themselves, as well as additional ideas for implementation, at jtayloreducation.com. They have the icons available in a JPEG format and so many resources to consider and use. They even have a Google Extension available for both educators and learners that can be used in so many ways. Go ahead, put the book down, and take a look around their website. J. Taylor Education is definitely the go-to resource when it comes to all things Depth and Complexity.

Depth Icons

Language of the Discipline

Depth and Complexity Icons. Source: Gould and Madsen, © 1995. J. Taylor Education, © 2006. The Center for Depth and Complexity, © 2018. Depth and Complexity Framework, Kaplan and Gould, © 1994.

Language of the Discipline is exactly what it sounds like it is. It's the opportunity to utilize the language and vocabulary that experts utilize when discussing a particular topic or idea. I often think about math when I think about this icon. Instead of using the word diamond, many educators prefer that their learners use the correct term for that shape, which is rhombus. Or I think about science. When talking about the metamorphosis of a butterfly, we often use the word cocoon when in reality cocoons are specific to moths, and chrysalises are formed by butterflies.

Language of the Discipline is a great way to extend the learning but it has to go beyond just writing words and their definitions...that's surface level. Remember, if we are considering Level 3 or 4 of Webb's Depth of Knowledge, we should be thinking about application. How can my learners use the Language of the Discipline icon to reach a deeper understanding of this concept, idea, or standard? Let me give you an example.

I taught fourth-grade Texas History and within that unit of study, my learners were expected to learn and understand the branches of government. Just because they were able to list the branches of government and regurgitate the description of each one did not mean that they had a deep understanding of how the government within our state was organized and how it worked.

If this is something that I felt like a student had already learned and understood, I was ready to provide an extension. To make this happen, I might find a way for them to actually use the Language of the Discipline regarding the Texas government to *do* something. I might challenge them to consider something that they would like to see become a law. Then, I would ask them to design a video game, using Scratch (scratch.mit.edu), to explain how a bill becomes a law utilizing the correct vocabulary and Language of the Discipline to explain how that bill moves through the branches of the Texas government. Do you see the difference? Not only did I make the experience personal by asking them to consider something they would like to see become a law, but I also challenged them to utilize the icon to create and design something that represented their understanding of the vocabulary.

Details

Depth and Complexity Icons. Source: Gould and Madsen, © 1995. J. Taylor Education, © 2006. The Center for Depth and Complexity, © 2018. Depth and Complexity Framework, Kaplan and Gould, © 1994.

I often say that I am not a detail-oriented person, and the same is true for many of our learners. When I think about gifted learners, I recognize that while many of them are able to pay attention to and remember specific details, many of them are big-picture thinkers and find it very difficult to recognize details. However, noticing and giving details are skills that can be practiced and utilized in many different ways.

As we've talked about throughout this book, it is not enough to simply explain what details are or how you expect them to be used. Instead, it's important that we give our learners the opportunity to pay attention to details through an authentic experience with purpose or provide details with a specific purpose in mind. In order to make this happen, I often try to think of my own experiences. When have I had to utilize details or when I have seen my own children at home utilize details to accomplish a goal?

I instantly think about the times that my husband and I have purchased furniture or toys that needed to be put together. Because I am not detail-oriented, I tend to skip over steps, resulting in a product that either can't be used or has to be rebuilt. Let's consider this idea from a math perspective. If your students are learning how to measure and are ready to move beyond the surface-level learning and into deep understanding, you might have them build something with very specific measurements. In doing so, it will be necessary for them to consider the details in order to be successful.

To take this one step further, you might have your learners polish up their writing skills by creating an expository writing piece for their peers. You could challenge another learner to follow the directions that are shared to determine if there were enough details given and if they were given in the order that would achieve the desired outcome.

Trends

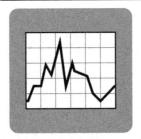

Depth and Complexity Icons. Source: Gould and Madsen, © 1995. J. Taylor Education, © 2006. The Center for Depth and Complexity, © 2018. Depth and Complexity Framework, Kaplan and Gould, © 1994.

Trends involve patterns, cause-and-effect relationships, and influences over time. These are often closely connected with what is learned in a social-studies or history classroom. However, if we take the time to really consider our content from this perspective, this icon can be utilized within a variety of content areas.

Using this icon provides us the opportunity to make real connections to pop culture and what is happening or has happened beyond the walls of the classroom. Anytime that we are able to make this a reality, there is a great likelihood that our learners will engage and invest in what is being learned.

In English Language Arts, our learners are often reading about and imagining settings and plots that are happening during a time period other than their own. Sometimes, it can be difficult for them to understand why specific characters look the way that they look or behave the way that they behave.

One way to encourage a deep understanding of the characters within a story or book is to give learners the opportunity to create a character analysis. In doing so, they might specifically be asked to compare the tendencies of a character with themselves or contrast the societal influences of the time period in the story with the present-day influences that we experience each and every day. If through this experience, learners are given the opportunity to focus on the trends from specific time periods, they will better understand not just who a character is and what they do, but also why they are who they are.

Patterns

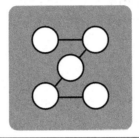

Depth and Complexity Icons. Source: Gould and Madsen, © 1995. J. Taylor Education, © 2006. The Center for Depth and Complexity, © 2018. Depth and Complexity Framework, Kaplan and Gould, © 1994.

I'm going to be honest...it's easy for me to get Patterns and Trends confused simply because trends involve patterns. If it's easy for me to confuse, it can be easy for your learners to confuse as well. This simply means that you will want to be explicit when talking about the difference and explaining each icon to your learners.

The Patterns icon encourages learners to recognize and identify repeating elements within a concept, idea, or standard. In order to use this icon to the depth that is required to demonstrate deep understanding, it's important to consider what patterns look like within the content that you teach and how those patterns can help learners think deeper about what is being learned.

There are so many patterns in science. Patterns can be easily woven into science labs as students are considering how to conduct an experiment. It's a good idea to consider how we might be able to utilize the patterns in science to help our learners think differently about the hypotheses that they create. Ask them to identify and consider any patterns that they can recognize regarding the idea or standard that they are exploring. Then, encourage them to take those patterns into consideration when writing their hypothesis for the experiment that they are currently conducting. You might even make this part of the process by asking, "What, if any, patterns led you to your hypothesis?"

Rules

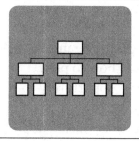

Depth and Complexity Icons. Source: Gould and Madsen, © 1995. J. Taylor Education, © 2006. The Center for Depth and Complexity, © 2018. Depth and Complexity Framework, Kaplan and Gould, © 1994.

Rules help learners understand that sometimes, things are the way that they are because of mandates, laws, and rules. This icon often involves anything that relates to structure, classification, or order. Gifted learners often like to ask why things are the way that they are. They want an explanation for something that they consider unfair, unjust, or opposite of what they think should be the case.

Let's take something that is fairly lighthearted and consider how we might give our learners the opportunity to think a little deeper by utilizing this icon. Have you ever played the game UNO? I think utilizing games in the classroom is always a good idea and most of the time, games require us to follow "the rules."

I remember teaching probability in my classroom and oftentimes, the concept was difficult for my learners to understand if they couldn't connect it to something that they had experienced. However, UNO is a game that many of our learners know how to play and it's a great way to introduce probability. Here's what that might look like…

1. Give your learners an opportunity to read the rules of the game.
2. Allow them to play the game so that everyone has a clear understanding of how to play.
3. Give learners the opportunity to sort the cards by color, number, or type.
4. Ask them to answer questions like, "What is the probability that you will pick up a 3?"; "How likely are you to pick up a green card?"; "What are the chances that you will draw a WILD card?"

One way to utilize the Rules icon to deepen this experience would be to consider how they might re-write the rules of the game. You might say, "How would you re-write the rules of the game to increase the probability of a player drawing a WILD card?" While there will be lots of ideas for them to consider, at the very least this will encourage them to think critically about probability and how small actions can increase or decrease the likelihood of something happening.

Unanswered Questions

Depth and Complexity Icons. Source: Gould and Madsen, © 1995. J. Taylor Education, © 2006. The Center for Depth and Complexity, © 2018. Depth and Complexity Framework, Kaplan and Gould, © 1994.

I love the Unanswered Questions icon, mostly because it's the icon that sometimes made my learners the most uncomfortable. You see, gifted learners like for their questions to be answered. In fact, they usually like to be the ones providing the answers. I think it's important that we give them opportunities to acknowledge and accept that they do not know the answers to everything and it's okay for questions to be unanswered.

One way to make this a reality in the classroom is to use the QFT, question formulation technique, that I shared in Chapter 4. This makes it absolutely necessary for learners to consider the questions that they have regarding a specific concept, idea, or standard and takes away the opportunity to share what they already know.

In my book, *Genius Hour: Passion Projects That Ignite Innovation and Student Inquiry*, I shared the KWHLAQ strategy that I learned about from Paul Solarz. I also read about this strategy on the Langwitches website (2020). I love utilizing this strategy as bookends for a learning experience.

At the beginning of a learning experience, you ask your learners three questions:

K—What do you KNOW?
W—What do you WANT to know?
H—HOW do you want to find out?

As you can see, this part of the experience encourages them to ask questions by asking them what they want to know. In answering this question, they are being put into a position that requires them to be self-aware enough to consider what they already know and what they don't.

The second part of this strategy can be utilized at the end of a learning experience. This involves asking learners to answer the following questions:

L—What did you LEARN?
A—What ACTION will you or did you take?
Q—What QUESTIONS do you still have?

Again, learners are given the opportunity to identify and share the questions that they still have. This helps them understand that they are not expected to know everything that there is to know about what has been learned and that it's okay to have unanswered questions.

Ethics

Depth and Complexity Icons. Source: Gould and Madsen, © 1995. J. Taylor Education, © 2006. The Center for Depth and Complexity, © 2018. Depth and Complexity Framework, Kaplan and Gould, © 1994.

This icon involves identifying and understanding the difference between right and wrong. What's fair and what's not? While this can be a tricky icon to implement, it gives our learners the opportunity to hear different perspectives and consider how they feel about controversial topics that matter.

Learning how to defend how they feel about a specific issue or decision that is made is an important skill that learners need to understand. They also need to learn how to respectfully disagree with someone. Too often, today's learners see on social media and read in the news how a disagreement leads to extreme situations that do not work toward a solution.

Consider how you might utilize this icon to encourage a deep understanding. Think about some of the novels that your learners are expected to read throughout the school year or the events that they learn about in World History. So often, they read the novel or learn about the events and are then simply asked to remember dates, facts, settings, and plots.

Diving deeper with this icon might involve your learners writing a faux opinion piece or op-ed about an event that happened in a book that resulted in a controversial outcome or a historical event that they think should have gone differently from an ethical perspective. In their writing, they should share why something should or should not have happened and defend the reasoning for their stance.

Big Idea

Depth and Complexity Icons. Source: Gould and Madsen, © 1995. J. Taylor Education, © 2006. The Center for Depth and Complexity, © 2018. Depth and Complexity Framework, Kaplan and Gould, © 1994.

As far as depth goes, the Big Idea icon is the deepest level of thought encouraged by the icons. Big ideas are often difficult for learners to consider, especially if they are accustomed to surface-level learning. This type of thinking requires learners to make connections and see the learning experience as so much more than just content that needs to be learned.

When I think about this icon, I often think about essential questions. In their book, *Understanding by Design Professional Development Workbook*, Jay McTighe and Grant Wiggins explain that "essential questions are designed to provoke and sustain student inquiry" (2006). They often do not have a right answer and cannot be Googled. Instead, they require learners to consider patterns and connections and make inferences based on what they know and what they want to know.

Giving learners an opportunity to consider the big idea of a learning experience is a wonderful way to add depth and extend learning. One example might be asking learners to utilize art to demonstrate the big idea of what was learned in class. They might draw a picture, write a poem, or perform a song to share their big idea with others. This type of experience allows learners to be creative and think beyond just sharing what they know through pencil and paper.

Complexity Icons

While considering depth is important, it's also important to think about complexity when designing an extension experience. Complexity encourages learners to think critically and understand a concept or idea by considering multiple perspectives, changes over time, and how it applies across disciplines.

Multiple Perspectives

Depth and Complexity Icons. Source: Gould and Madsen, © 1995. J. Taylor Education, © 2006. The Center for Depth and Complexity, © 2018. Depth and Complexity Framework, Kaplan and Gould, © 1994.

This is another one of my favorite icons because I think it's so important. Being able to see a situation or idea from multiple perspectives is an extremely valuable skill both inside and outside of the classroom. We've all been in a situation in which someone wasn't willing to see something from a different perspective and that can be a very frustrating experience.

Asking our learners to consider something from someone else's perspective gives them the opportunity to practice empathy and an open mindset. This icon can be used to ask learners to think about a situation from a specific person or a specific group's perspective. In doing so, they are encouraged to think beyond themselves.

Perspective is "a particular attitude toward or way of regarding something; a point of view." Dr. Michelle Borba has shared that

> When children can grasp another's perspective, they are more likely to be empathetic, anticipate other's behavior or thinking, handle conflicts peacefully, be less judgmental, value differences, speak up for those who are victimized, and act in ways that are more helpful, comforting, and supportive of others.
>
> *(Borba, 2018)*

Isn't this what we want for our learners? If you weren't considering making Multiple Perspectives a priority in your classroom before, my hope is that the quote from Dr. Borba helps you realize the incredible impact that this can have on every learner.

Normally, when we think about perspectives, we think about people. However, thinking beyond that idea and encouraging learners to consider the perspective of an inanimate object can result in a meaningful critical thinking experience. Take surfing for example. It's fairly easy to think about the surfer's experience. Show a video of surfers to your learners and ask them to write down what the surfers' perspective might be. What are they thinking? How are they feeling? How has their perspective changed from when they were paddling out into the ocean to when they stood up on the board and began riding the wave?

But what about the wave? What is the wave's perspective? If the ocean could think or talk, what might it be thinking? How would it feel? This experience encourages learners to think beyond themselves and people like them. They have to consider perspective in a different way and that requires them to think differently through a more complex learning experience that will result in deep understanding.

Across Disciplines

Depth and Complexity Icons. Source: Gould and Madsen, © 1995. J. Taylor Education, © 2006. The Center for Depth and Complexity, © 2018. Depth and Complexity Framework, Kaplan and Gould, © 1994.

I'm still amazed sometimes at the fact that we often teach content and subject areas in such silos. The reality is that beyond the walls of the classroom, none of us compartmentalize the work that we do into specific subjects. Instead, we often use our knowledge and experience from all of the content areas to solve problems and develop solutions.

The ability to approach a problem utilizing different content knowledge is one of the reasons that I am such a fan of project-based learning. Any time a learner can use the sum of their knowledge to solve a problem, I simply think that it's the best way to learn.

Oftentimes, I think it's easy to stay focused on a particular content area, as educators, because it's what we've been hired to do. While I know so many wonderful educators that intentionally weave additional content into what they teach, the reality is that for the most part, school still isn't intentionally designed to prioritize the collaboration that would give educators the opportunity to design with this in mind.

Consider the perspective of a 30,0000-foot view. Oftentimes, when I am flying out of Dallas and I look out of the window, I am able to see things from the air that I would be unable to see or recognize from the street view. For example, I might be able to see that several houses in one neighborhood have pools in their backyards or I might be able to see how different streets connect different parts of a neighborhood. I would be unable to notice those things if I were simply walking down the street.

I often think about this as an example of why it's important that we are willing to collaborate with other disciplines and consider the standards that are taught in other classrooms. It gives us the 30,000-foot view that we need to make connections, see what we can work together to achieve, and understand the big picture.

I'm not suggesting that the street view isn't important, I'm just suggesting that if that's the only view that we are willing to consider, we are missing important opportunities for across-disciplines connections.

When giving learners the opportunity to extend what they've already learned about a specific concept, idea, or standard, it's a good idea to ask them to consider what has been learned from the perspective of a different content area. How could math be used to explain the metamorphosis of a butterfly? How might we utilize science vocabulary to explain a historical event? Is it going to require them to think differently and beyond what might make them comfortable? Yes. Will it result in a much more authentic and deeper learning experience? Absolutely.

Changes Over Time

Depth and Complexity Icons. Source: Gould and Madsen, © 1995. J. Taylor Education, © 2006. The Center for Depth and Complexity, © 2018. Depth and Complexity Framework, Kaplan and Gould, © 1994.

This icon encourages learners to think beyond what is happening right now and instead, consider how something has changed over time.

I recently visited the Pioneer Museum in Fredericksburg, Texas. In doing so, I stepped into the past to experience what life was like so many years ago. Throughout our tour, I was reminded of how innovation has changed the way that we live and work every single day. And then, I stepped into a one-room schoolhouse. As I stood in that space and considered what learning looked like so long ago, I realized that there are so many things that we could learn from that experience. I actually asked on social media what others thought might surprise educators from that time about what education looks like today. One of the responses shared that they might be surprised at how overwhelmed we are with the idea of differentiation. I mean, think about it, the one-room schoolhouse was the epitome of effective differentiation. These classrooms often had a single teacher that would have students in first through eighth grade. The number of learners ranged from six to 40 or more and the teacher was expected to teach them all (*One-room schoolhouse*, n.d.).

Look, I'm not suggesting that things haven't changed, and I fully realize that expectations that are placed on today's educators far exceed the expectations that were placed on those so long ago. In fact, the differentiation that today's educators are expected to provide is probably very different from the differentiation that was provided long ago. However, I think it's important to consider and learn what we can from those that came before us. Similarly, I would imagine the teachers from that time would be willing to admit that there is a lot that they could learn from us as well.

This is a perfect example of changes over time. In order to truly understand what differentiation looked like then and what it looks like now, we must use our critical thinking skills to compare and contrast experiences. This is an idea that you can utilize in your classroom to extend a learning experience. Ask your learners to consider how an idea that is being learned about in class might have been received in the past or how it might be received in the future. Ask them to justify their response and possibly even create a presentation that can be shared with their peers.

Technology Tools

I often like to find tools and resources that will give learners the opportunities to utilize several or all of the Depth and Complexity Icons. I think these provide a meaningful opportunity for learners that finish their work early or have already mastered what's being taught.

One of those tools is Virtual Vacation (virtualvacation.us). I absolutely love this resource as a way to give learners an opportunity to see things from different perspectives, recognize and utilize details, understand patterns beyond the walls of the classroom, and so much more. Virtual Vacation allows learners to take a walking, driving, or flying tour in a new place. They can visit Paris, Moscow, and San Francisco...amazing, right?

My favorite piece on this website is called City Guesser. This particular part of the website allows learners to utilize what they know and their inferencing strategies to make an educated guess as to where they are in the world. They have to pay attention to details, consider unanswered questions, and possibly even learn new words to make a prediction and get as close as possible to the correct destination. It is so much fun and I'm warning you now...it's also super addictive.

Wonderopolis (wonderopolis.org) is also a great resource. This a tool that I've talked about in every book that I've written. It gives learners an opportunity to be curious and explore specific topics through accessing and learning from a Wonder of the Day. Learners can read the Wonder of the Day or they can search the wonders for something that they would like to learn. In doing so, they are introduced to new vocabulary (Language of the Discipline) and given opportunities to dive deeper into topics as they learn by doing. While at first glance, this might not seem like an opportunity to reach a deeper understanding,

I think that if we are intentional about weaving the icons into this experience, it can definitely provide depth and can encourage learners to think about a topic from a new perspective.

Genius Hour and the Icons

I don't want to wrap this chapter up without acknowledging that passion-based learning or Genius Hour can be a meaningful way to extend learning and deepen understanding. Giving learners an opportunity to explore their own passions and interests while making an impact on the world around them just makes sense. I love the idea of introducing the Genius Hour process (passion, plan, pitch, project, product, and presentation) (McNair, 2022) to your learners and then letting their projects run in the background. In other words, any time they finish their work early, they will have the project waiting to be worked on.

The Depth and Complexity Icons can easily be woven into this process. For example, as learners become experts on specific topics and ideas, they will need to utilize the Language of the Discipline to share their ideas with others. When pitching their idea to the class, they will be asked to consider the perspective of their peers as they listen to and provide feedback. There are so many ways that the icons can be woven into this experience and utilizing this as an extension can give educators a big return on their investment.

So, what do you think? Could these icons help you extend and enrich a learning experience in a meaningful way? You can utilize them in so many ways and they are very versatile, making them manageable to implement in any grade level or content area. I hope that you learn to love these icons and the power that they have in the classroom as much as I did. Take some time to explore and consider how you might be able to make this work with your learners. I think that you will be glad that you did.

Reflection Questions

1. After reading about Marcy's experience with the Depth and Complexity Icons as well as my own, what are you still wondering?

2. Which of the icons do you think will benefit your learners the most?

3. Do you think that these icons will help you be more intentional about the extensions that you provide for your learners that have already mastered what is being learned or finish their work early?

What is your biggest takeaway from Chapter 8?

_____

_____

_____

What challenged or validated something that you already knew?

_____

_____

_____

Works Cited

Borba, M. (2018, 2 October). *7 ways to teach perspective taking and stretch students' empathy muscles.* The Robert D. and Billie Ray Center. Retrieved 18 May, 2022, from raycenter.wp.drake.edu/2018/10/02/perspective-taking/.

Kaplan, S., & Gould, B. (1994). *Depth and complexity framework.*

Gould, M. (1995). *Depth and complexity icons.* J Taylor Education, 2006. The Center for Depth & Complexity, 2018.

Gould, J. (2019, 25 March). *J Taylor Education's newest depth & complexity product - TALK cards.* J Taylor Education. Retrieved from https://www.jtayloreducation.com/newest-j-tayloreducation-depth-complexity-products-talk-cards/.

Griffith, M. (n.d.). *Depth and complexity and content imperatives.* Envision Gifted. Retrieved 18 May, 2022, from envisiongifted.com/services/.

McNair, A. (2022). *Genius hour: Passion projects that ignite innovation and student inquiry* (2nd ed.). Routledge.

McTighe, J., & Wiggins, G.P. (2006). *Understanding by design professional development workbook.* Hawker Brownlow Education.

One-room schoolhouse. (n.d.). www.americaslibrary.gov. Retrieved 18 May, 2022, from www.americaslibrary.gov/es/ny/esnyschool1.html#:~:text=In%20the%2019th%20and%20early.

Usage of the KWHLAQ: Upgrade your KWL chart to the 21st century. (2020, 9 January). Langwitches: The Magic of Learning. Retrieved 17 May, 2022, from langwitches.org/blog/2020/01/09/upgrade-your-kwl-chart-to-the-21st-century-introduction/.

Chapter 9

Providing Extra Support through Encouragement

BIG IDEA

Every learner will need extra support at some point and it's important that we are purposeful about the intervention that is provided.

DOI: 10.4324/9781003349471-13

127

Just because a learner is gifted doesn't mean that they won't struggle, and just because they struggle doesn't mean that they aren't gifted. The same is true for struggling learners. The majority of them will not struggle every day. There will be things that they understand and things that they don't understand. Giving them an opportunity to be honest about this will create a classroom culture of transparency and support. This is why I am so supportive of flexible grouping and the impact that it can have in the classroom and on our learners.

Finally, the most important part of designing for depth is considering what learners will do if they need *extra support*, or what I like to call encouragement. While the reality is that we often consider how we will meet the needs of the learners that struggle, I'm not sure that we often consider how meaningful that extra support is and whether or not it will give us a return on our investment.

Laird Hamilton, an American big-wave surfer, once said, "Wiping out is an underappreciated skill" (SurferToday.com, n.d.). I love that statement so much and it's such a great way for a learner that doesn't understand to approach whatever it is that is challenging them. Instead, we often see struggle or failure in the classroom as a negative experience that is either a result of the content not being taught well or not being understood well. I just don't think it's always that simple.

Did you know that surfers experience different types of wipeouts? Some are minor, some are major, but the reality is that any wipeout can discourage a surfer from wanting to get back on the board. The same is true for our learners when they struggle in the classroom. Gifted learners can especially experience this as a result of the unrealistic expectations that they are often operating under.

It can be difficult for gifted learners to acknowledge that they need extra support and even more difficult to accept that extra support when it is being given. However, it is so important for them to understand and recognize that we all have both strengths and weaknesses and our weaknesses do not make us "less gifted."

When we are thinking about how to provide extra support for our learners, I think it's important to do so through encouragement. There are two definitions of encouragement which I think make so much sense when it comes to supporting them when they don't understand or struggle to think beyond the surface level.

1. The action of giving someone support, confidence, or hope.
2. Persuasion to do or to continue something.

It can be tempting to want to come to the rescue when our learners struggle or don't understand. I know that in my classroom, I often felt like a terrible teacher when my learners struggled. I felt like it was my fault. After all, they were gifted learners. If I couldn't teach in a way that they could understand, what was I even doing?

But, it is a much better idea for us, as educators, to support, provide confidence, and help our learners find hope in even the most difficult of situations. Persuading them to continue to work through something even when it's hard is as much a part of our jobs as teaching specific standards and designing experiences that will make learning meaningful.

When a surfer falls off of the board, I do not imagine that the instructor swims out to meet them and props them back up on the board. Instead, they probably shout things from the shore like, "You can do this!" or "I believe in you!" They fully recognize that once the surfer is out on the waves, it's time for them to utilize their own devices to accomplish what it is that they paddled out to do...ride the waves. There may be specific instructions that they provide when the surfer returns to the shore, but they recognize that at that moment, the best learning that the surfer can experience is by doing.

The Power of Productive Struggle

I learned a while back that butterflies struggle as they emerge from their chrysalis. Through a little research and digging, I found a wonderful blog post from Lee-Anne Ragan, M.Ed., B.S.W., that helped me understand exactly why this is and it made even more sense. In her blog post titled "What We Can Learn from a Butterfly's Struggle to Escape Its Chrysalis," she shares that, "Butterflies, as it turns out, release a chemical when they're getting out of their chrysalis, a chemical that strengthens their wings. Their movements inside the chrysalis pump fluid into their wings, which help the wings expand" (Ragan, 2019). In other words, without the movements that happen during the struggle of emerging from the chrysalis, they simply wouldn't be able to fly beyond that extremely limiting environment.

I know for a fact that there were times in my classroom when I took away the struggle from my learners because it made me feel like a better teacher. But the reality is that, in doing so, I was preventing them from being able to spread their wings and fly beyond the walls of the classroom. Now that I know what I know now, I fully realize and recognize that this can be devastating to our learners.

Instead, it's important that we help them see the struggle as part of the learning experience and give them the support that they need to work through that struggle to emerge as the beautiful butterflies that we know that they are. I believe that we can do this by giving them the confidence and support that they need every single day.

A surfer that isn't confident probably isn't going to get right back on the board after a major wipeout. They might be embarrassed, afraid of getting hurt, or they might not believe enough in themselves to even attempt a second ride. Confidence plays a big role in a learner's willingness to get back on the board and ride the waves again even after falling off...maybe more than once.

Types of Support

Direct instruction is not a bad idea when done well. You will have learners in your classroom who will understand a concept through application and those that will learn it through hearing it explained well. When a student doesn't understand, it's never a bad idea to be even more explicit in your approach. The key to direct instruction being effective is being realistic about the attention span of your learners. If what is being explained is going to be lengthy, it's a good idea to chunk it up into smaller sections so that they grasp what is being shared.

Giving learners the opportunity to collaborate is also a great way to provide extra support. I recently saw a video on Facebook of a turtle that had turned over on its back in a pool of shallow water. As it struggled, the other turtles came to the rescue and worked together to get it turned back over and swimming again. This reminded me of what collaboration should look like. When a learner is struggling, giving his peers that understand an opportunity to share their approach to the learning can be very valuable.

I want to be clear, I'm not talking about peer tutoring. To be honest, I'm not a huge fan of peer tutoring because, too often, it's utilized in a way that doesn't benefit either learner. Instead, it's used to move things along or substitute for the work that we, as teachers, should be doing. The difference is this...a learner being asked to teach another student because the teacher doesn't have time is not okay. However, if a learner is being asked to collaborate with another learner to help them understand, and in doing so, they, themselves, reach a deeper understanding of the content, this is when this type of peer-to-peer learning can be valuable.

The bottom line is that extra support can be extremely valuable when done well. However, just like everything else that we have discussed in this book, the extra support that we design as part of a learning experience has to be intentional. Let's spend a little time focusing on the power of intervention, what it looks like when it's done well, and what it looks like when it's not.

Effective Intervention

I've recently thought a lot about effective intervention for gifted learners. This topic hits close to home and is important to me for personal reasons. You see, my daughter is gifted but often struggles within the traditional school system. She sometimes needs intervention in order to make connections and make progress in a way that makes sense to her. I think it's important to have very real conversations about what this should and should not look like.

The Edvocate shares that "classroom intervention is a set of steps a teacher takes to help a child improve in their area of need by removing educational barriers" (Lynch, 2019). I think the next question becomes, "What does effective intervention look like?" There are so many ways to effectively implement intervention when a learner does not understand. However, I think that we have to be honest about what will and will not work so that we don't feel as if we are spending time doing something that will not provide a return on our investment.

Effective Intervention Is Intentional

Intervention must be done with intention. Every child is different and requires different strategies and solutions in order for intervention to work. It's important that we are intentional about *why* and *how* intervention is being provided.

When a surgeon is operating on a patient, they never randomly choose what needs to be addressed. There is a diagnosis and ultimately, a strategy put into place so that the surgery that takes place will produce the desired outcome. The same should be true for intervention. We have to know exactly what needs to be learned and why it's not being understood. Is it a possibility that in order to learn, we need to consider a different strategy, a different voice, or a different motivation?

A different strategy can be considered if students are simply not learning the concept, idea, or standard in the way that it is being taught. Doing the same type of intervention at a different time of day makes no sense. If a learner is unable to understand, it's important to consider alternative ways to help them make connections to learn in a way that makes sense for them.

Sometimes, they simply need to hear it said in a different way. I can think of many times that one or two of my students just couldn't "hear" it from me. For whatever reason, the way that I was teaching the content or asking them to learn the content just didn't click. Allowing our learners to experience learning from someone else's perspective can sometimes help them understand and make important connections. That voice might be that of a peer, an outside expert, or another educator.

Finally, we may need to explore a different form of motivation. Remember the three different types of motivation (autonomy, mastery, and purpose)? These should be considered and focused on when what is being learned isn't being understood. If a learner isn't driven through mastery, the intrinsic motivation to get better, maybe we need to focus on purpose, using that skill to accomplish something bigger or create change. Or, maybe we need to provide more autonomy, more choice, and more opportunity for students to self-direct in order to learn a particular strategy or skill. I'm not suggesting that we make the intervention optional, I'm simply suggesting that we give them the opportunity to have a voice in what their invention looks like.

Effective Intervention Is Interactive

I believe that intervention is a two-way street. While it's important for us, as educators, to facilitate and help our learners understand, it's also important for them to invest and provide the feedback that we need to make decisions.

Intervention can be made interactive by making formative assessment a priority. Frequent check-ins and clear communication are important to help us know if the intervention that is being provided is working or if we need to consider alternative solutions.

Being self-aware is an important SEL skill that our learners need to practice. Give them the opportunity to practice this skill by asking them how they feel throughout a learning experience. As mentioned in an earlier chapter, I like the idea of providing a scale and asking learners to rate how well they understand what is being learned.

I do want to take this opportunity to suggest that we not encourage learners to use emojis to demonstrate their level of understanding. Too often, I have seen the sad face emoji used to convey the message that a student doesn't understand. It's not sad that they don't understand, and sending that message will make it difficult for students to value productive struggle. They will find it difficult to admit when they don't understand simply because the emoji makes it seem negative when nothing could be further from the truth.

The definition of interactive is "two people or things influencing or having an effect on each other." If we want to have an effect on our learners, we have to intentionally understand where they are and what they need. We should affect their learning through providing effective instruction and intervention. They should affect our instruction by providing the feedback that we need in order to do so.

Effective Intervention Is Impactful

If intervention isn't impactful, then it's a waste of time. If what is being done or learned during an intervention time doesn't leave an impact, our learners will forget what has been learned as soon as they walk out of the door. We ultimately have to understand who they are, what they enjoy, and how they learn to impact them. Otherwise, it can feel like a waste of time, which will result in frustration for both the educator and the learner.

Sometimes, learning can happen through direct teaching or explicit instruction. Other times, learning needs to happen through doing. Regardless of how we make it happen, remember, we should be asking how they will learn rather than how we will teach. And the reality is that doing the same thing every day, such as sitting in front of a computer answering question after question, will not result in true understanding of a concept or standard.

In order for the intervention to be effective, we should consider what is being learned and why it is not being understood. Is it because there is a lack of prior knowledge? Is the learner missing necessary foundational pieces? Why was the original opportunity to learn ineffective?

The bottom line is that if we want intervention to have an impact we must ask ourselves, "How will they learn this particular concept or standard?" "What do I need to do as the educator and what do they need to do as the learner?" Asking these questions prioritizes the learning and helps us remember that simply because our students hear it, see it, or even do it, that doesn't mean that they understood it.

What Effective Intervention Is Not

While it's important to consider what effective intervention is, I think it's just as important to consider what it is not.

Effective Intervention Is Not Immeasurable

Intervention with no data cannot be effective. In order to know if what we are doing is working, it's important to check in often, collect data, and make decisions based on that data. Data should be used as a tool to diagnose where students are and what they will need going forward.

Simply creating an intervention time and providing assignments for students to work on during that time will not move the needle. Instead, we must collaborate to look at what students are doing, where they are in their journey, and what tools we need to add to their backpacks to help them progress.

Measuring the impact that intervention has on our learners helps us continue to make progress. When there is no progress, there will be frustration. Intentional intervention with meaningful data can make a huge difference in a learner's experience and willingness to invest.

Effective Intervention Is Not Irrelevant

Just like anything else that we do in the classroom, the methods that we put in place must be meaningful. This means that we have to know our learners well. Think back to the grocery store analogy that I shared in Chapter 3. Sometimes, they are putting it back on their shelf because they don't understand why it needs to be in their basket.

Just like everything else that we have talked about throughout this book, intervention has to be relevant. If it's not, we are simply giving them things that will not stick with them. Consider making things relevant through personal connections, relatable stories, and student-driven experiences.

Effective Intervention Is Not Insulting

Learners shouldn't feel like intervention is a negative experience. Instead, they should understand that very few learners understand everything and it is likely that, at some point, everyone will require some form of intervention. It might sound silly, but I think it's important to be creative and innovative with how we refer to intervention time during the school day.

Many schools refer to this time as WIN (What I Need) Time. I like this because it speaks to the reality that learners may need different things on different days. Some days, they might need extra support, other days they might need enrichment. However, if we are going to call that time What I Need, it's important that we are intentional about making that time about what our students actually need and not what we think they need, assume they need, or wish they needed.

It's insulting to make intervention about rules and timelines. Even if that is the reality, possibly because of the result of a standardized test, we still have to find ways to intentionally focus on real goals and meaningful outcomes of an intervention program. In doing so, I think we will help our learners realize that if intervention is part of their day, that simply means that they are being given an opportunity to reach a deeper understanding and become better at learning.

When we begin really consider what intervention is and is not, it will no longer be about getting the correct answer, but instead, our learners will begin to think about thinking and truly recognize the power of deep understanding.

Reflection Questions

1. How would you describe effective intervention?

2. How would you describe ineffective innovation?

3. How do your gifted learners react when they don't understand, and how you can help them recognize that it's okay to struggle?

What is your biggest takeaway from Chapter 9?

_____

_____

_____

What challenged or validated something that you already knew?

_____

_____

_____

Works Cited

Effective intervention: What it is and is not. (2021, 24 August). A Meaningful Mess. Retrieved 17 May, 2022, from www.andimcnair.com/andis-blog/intervention-what-it-is-and-is-not.

Lynch, M. (2019, 15 October). *Types of classroom interventions.* The Edvocate. Retrieved 17 May, 2022, from www.theedadvocate.org/types-of-classroom-interventions/#:~:text=In%20general%20terms%2C%20classroom%20intervention.

Ragan, L.-A. (2019, 15 October). *What we can learn from a butterfly's struggle to escape its chrysalis.* Rock Paper Scissors. Retrieved 17 May, 2022, from rockpaperscissorsinc.com/what-we-can-learn-from-a-butterflys-struggle-to-escape-its-chrysalis/.

SurferToday.com, Editor at. (n.d.). *The Best quotes by Laird Hamilton.* Surfertoday. Retrieved from www.surfertoday.com/surfing/the-best-quotes-by-laird-hamilton#:~:text=Just%20because%20people%20are%20doing.

Chapter 10

Creating the Perfect Wave

BIG IDEA

As educators, it's imperative that we help our students see learning as more than passing grades and perfect attendance. Learning is a life-long process that will serve them well for the rest of their lives.

DOI: 10.4324/9781003349471-14

141

Throughout the chapters of the book, I've shared a lot of information and details that I believe we have to start to consider in order to make learning meaningful for today's gifted learners. While I hope that you have enjoyed every part of the book and that you are able to practically implement much of what has been shared, I hope that you will also see the big picture… designing for depth will help all of our learners move beyond the shore, get on their boards, and ride the waves.

Considering User Experience

"User experience (UX) design is the process design teams use to create products that provide meaningful and relevant experiences to users" (Interaction Design Foundation, 2019). This idea is often used by businesses when considering how valuable their products will be to their customer base or gamers when determining how players will interact with the game.

Those that work in the area of user design focus on the why, the what, and the how of whatever it is that they are researching. Their goal is ultimately to make sure that the product is not only engaging but meaningful and relevant to those that will be using it. The user experience is something that we should consider as educators. If we can recognize that ultimately, our learners are the users when it comes to the learning experiences we design, this begins to make a lot of sense.

As I continued to research this idea and read about what user experience experts do, I came across and began to learn about the UX Pyramid (*Every designer should know the UX design pyramid with the user needs*, 2018). This tool helps those who design consider whether or not the product will be received well within the community that it is being created for. I found it interesting that, first of all, the pyramid was divided into two categories—objective and subjective categories. The bottom of the pyramid considers whether the product is functional and usable while the top of the pyramid focuses on how engaging it will be for the user.

This is similar to the ideas that I've shared in Chapter 2 of this book. We must consider the practicality of what it is that we are trying to do in the classroom, but we must also consider it as an experience for the learner and whether or not it will be significant enough for them to engage.

Usability.gov explains that "user experience (UX) focuses on having a deep understanding of users, what they need, what they value, their abilities, and also their limitations" (Usability .gov, 2019). If that doesn't sound exactly like what we should be doing as educators, I don't know what does. If we took the time to focus on these things, the school experience would become so much more meaningful. It only makes sense that we take time to learn from this industry and consider how we can utilize some of their ideas to change the way that we design experiences for the learners that sit in today's classrooms.

Design Labs

As I think about putting all of the pieces together and designing experiences that are both manageable and meaningful, I began to wonder what it would look like if every campus had a dedicated space for educators to design experiences for their learners. I visit a lot of campuses and I've seen examples of these on campuses that are forward-thinking and proactive in their approach.

Design labs are often described as incubation spaces for ideas. Instead of sitting in isolation writing lesson plans, what if educators had a collaborative space with the tools, resources, and visual reminders that they needed to design—wait for it—meaningful experiences for today's learners?

One of the things that I often think about is how helpful it might be to have gifted/talented specialists sit in on teacher PLCs. While I know this is happening in some districts, I don't think it is the norm. When designing for depth, it's important that educators have experts to lean on and ask questions that will provide answers that they do not have and do not have the time to search out. Making this a priority will help educators better understand gifted learners and what they need in order to engage and empower them in the classroom.

I have a sneaky suspicion that administrators would be blown away by the impact that purposeful collaboration would have on the culture of a campus or district. Instead, often educators sit alone in isolation feeling as if they are the only ones struggling with ideas to engage and empower the learners that will walk into their classroom the next day. Just imagine how a design lab or incubation space might transform not only the teachers' experience but what learners experience as well. The space would likely be a catalyst for innovative solutions and cross-curricular collaborations that would have a huge impact on today's learners.

Let me give you a practical example of something that could be included in such a space. There might be a whiteboard space for educators to share what is and isn't working in their classrooms. This could be made even more intentional by providing a space for educators to share how they are engaging their learners as soon as they walk into class, how they are designing experiences that will leave an impression, and how they are empowering students to make connections. They could share ideas for meaningful differentiation through collaborating around ideas for extension and extra support...the possibilities are endless!

Creating Soul Surfers

Today's learners should look in the classroom the way that soul surfers look on the water. According to Wikipedia, a soul surfer is "a surfer who surfs for the sheer pleasure of surfing" (*Soul surfer*, 2021). What if our learners learned for the sheer pleasure of learning? What if instead of performing for grades or feeling as if they always had to focus on meeting their goals, they were given the opportunity to focus on growth?

According to Surfer Today, soul surfers also "feel the need to explore and search for uncharted waves" (SurferToday.com, 2021). It's safe to say that many of the learners that sit in today's classrooms have lost the need to explore and search for things that they do not know. They simply show up at school out of compliance and do the bare minimum to get by and receive the grades that will keep them out of trouble. And, if we're honest, many learners don't even do that.

Until we begin to design for depth and prioritize the parts of learning that are absolutely essential in order to make school a place that today's learners want to be, educators will continue to feel as if they are the ones doing all of the work. It will continue to feel like an uphill battle that is both frustrating and exhausting.

DMLE Framework

Throughout this book, I have described a framework that I believe is both manageable for educators and meaningful for today's learners. We have explored the importance and practical application of each piece of the framework and I hope that you have been able to see how utilizing different strategies and ideas can help you design an experience for depth that will ignite a willingness to invest from the students that sit in your classroom each and every day.

I'm not super creative, so I simply refer to this framework as the DMLE (Designing a Meaningful Learning Experience) Framework. If you would like access to the template as a PDF, please visit andimcnair.com/DMLE.

In recently sharing my framework, one of my colleagues mentioned the 5E Instructional Framework (Bybee and Landes, 1990). I had not taken a close look at this before and had not used it in my classroom. However, after looking at the model, I quickly realized that, in their design, they paved the way for so many new ideas and approaches regarding the way that educators lesson plan, or, better yet, design experiences. The 5E framework (Engage, Explore, Explain, Elaborate, Evaluate) was created to promote inquiry in the science classroom. While I did not consider this framework when I created my approach, it's clear that there are pieces of a learning experience that just make sense, regardless of the content that is being learned. I always want to honor and acknowledge the work that has been done before. So, after learning about their work and looking at the framework I wanted to share it here as an additional way to design experiences in the classroom.

That being said, the goal of the DMLE framework that I've shared throughout this book is to design an experience (engage, experience, and empower) with intentionality so that every learner is given the opportunity to understand the content in a way that makes sense. This part of the design is where we ignite a willingness to invest, provide an opportunity to learn, and encourage connections beyond the walls of the classroom. After the evidence is considered, we want to be intentional about how we provide what the learner needs…extra support or extension? Then, if planned well, the extension or extra support will provide clarity and/or depth, resulting in a real understanding of what has been learned.

If your school district requires you to utilize a specific template, I'm not suggesting that you replace that template with the one that I am sharing. However, I am suggesting that if the pieces themselves are not included, it might be important to have a conversation about how including them might have a positive impact on the learners in your classroom, on your campus, or in your district. For example, if the template that your district utilizes doesn't encourage educators to consider how the learning will be extended for learners that already understand, it might be important to ask if that piece can somehow be added in an effort to ensure that we are designing for every learner.

As far as implementing this within a district or on a campus, I think it's important to help educators understand that they don't have to be extremely detailed in each box as the intentionality is already there because the boxes exist. I believe that autonomy is important as educators design experiences for their learners. Just making it a priority to include each piece will impact the experiences that are designed and will help us consider more than just the content that has to be mastered each day.

It's a good idea to spend time on each piece of the framework to deeply understand why each piece is included and how it can be implemented. Doing so won't happen overnight but it will result in a much better understanding of the process and the impact that it can have on our learners in the classroom.

Final Thoughts

In closing, I want to encourage you to think differently about the way that we design experiences for today's learners. It's important that we do it for them but it's also important that we do it for ourselves. None of us want to feel as if we are wasting our time every day or that we not making any progress for our learners that need it the most.

Settling for mediocrity and surface-level learning is detrimental to our learners, and especially harmful to gifted learners that are begging to be challenged in the classroom. Gifted learners deserve the opportunity to show growth just like the other learners in the classroom. That will not happen if we aren't intentional about designing experiences that give them the opportunity to do so.

So, this is your invitation. Come on in, the water's great and the waves are even better. I am super stoked about what lies ahead for today's learners if we take the time to focus on creating the perfect wave. I'll grab my board if you'll grab yours. Let's do this...not because I think it's a good idea, but because it will result in school being a place that our learners want to be. And when that begins to happen, we will fully understand what learning can and should look like every single day. Surf's up!

Reflection Questions

1. What questions do you still have about the framework?

2. How might user experience impact the way that you design experiences?

3. What is your description of the perfect wave?

What is your biggest takeaway from Chapter 10?

_____

_____

_____

What challenged or validated something that you already knew?

_____

_____

_____

Works Cited

Bybee, R. & Landes, N.M. (1990). Science for life and living: An elementary school science program from Biological Sciences Improvement Study (BSCS). *The American Biology Teacher, 52*(2), 92–98.

Every designer should know the UX design pyramid with the user needs. (2018, 26 December). Syndicode - Custom Software Development Company. Retrieved May 17, 2022, from syndicode.com/blog/the-ux-design-pyramid-with-the-user-needs/.

Interaction Design Foundation. (2019). *What is user experience (UX) design?* Retrieved from www.interaction-design.org / literature/topics/ux-design.

Soul Surfer. (2021, 30 August). Wikipedia. Retrieved May 17, 2022, from en.wikipedia.org/wiki/Soulsurfer.

SurferToday.com, Editor at. (2021, 21 January). *12 signs you're a soul surfer.* Surfertoday. Retrieved 18 May, 2022, from www.surfertoday.com/surfing/signs-you-are-a-soul-surfer.

Usability.gov. (2019). *User experience basics.* Retrieved from https://www.usability.gov/what-and-why/user-experience.html.

Meet the Author

Andi McNair was a classroom teacher for 16 years before making the decision to leave the classroom to serve and support educators. After teaching general education for 13 years, she spent her last three years in the classroom serving gifted learners. After deciding to leave the classroom, Andi became a Digital Innovation Specialist and Gifted/Talented Specialist at ESC Region 12 and in 2016 she was named one of the Top People in Education to Watch by the Academy of Education Arts and Sciences. As a mom of gifted children, she found her passion in advocating for and designing experiences for gifted learners. Now, she enjoys helping educators all over the world do the same. Andi is married to her junior-high sweetheart. They live in a small Texas town where they have raised their children and enjoy spending time with friends. Andi absolutely loves sharing her passion for innovative education with other teachers who want more for their students. She is now an international speaker, consultant, author, and podcaster. To learn more or to invite Andi to speak at your organization, on your campus, or in your district, visit her website at www.andimcnair.com.

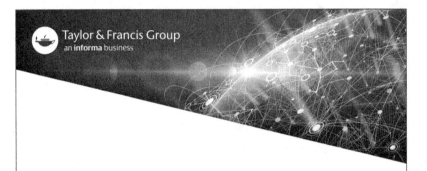

Printed in the United States
by Baker & Taylor Publisher Services